An Undoing

An Undoing

A Pastor's Story of Resilience

Matthew Hansen

WIPF & STOCK · Eugene, Oregon

Wipf & Stock
An Imprint of Wipf and Stock Publishers
199 W. 8th Ave., Suite 3
Eugene, OR 97401

www.wipfandstock.com

PAPERBACK ISBN: 978-1-5326-7595-9
HARDCOVER ISBN: 978-1-5326-7596-6
EBOOK ISBN: 978-1-5326-7597-3

Manufactured in the U.S.A.

To Sarah, the girl from Morocco, an image of the divine feminine. You make life more beautiful, the years more meaningful, and this journey more adventurous. I love you. Thank you for being you.

For the time being, your place is not here [church]. I give you my blessing for a great obedience in the world. You still have much journeying before you. You will have to endure everything before you come back again. And there will be much work to do. But I have no doubt of you, that is why I am sending you. Christ is with you. Keep him, and he will keep you.

—Elder Zosima[1]

1. Dostoyevsky, *Brothers Karamazov*, 77.

Contents

Preface

In life, if we are moving slowly enough, we all have different sorts of epiphanies, epiphanies that move us or cause us to move. In the pages to come, I mention several of my own personal epiphanies, and while many of them were more negative in nature, they were nonetheless epiphanies that were so powerful I couldn't shake them and they, in turn, became fuel for change in my own life.

The book you hold in your hands (or downloaded on your e-reader) is divided into two parts. The first portion of this book is the result of a haunting epiphany that came from a sermon I preached. Several years ago, some of the churches in Austin partnered with the larger atheist association. Much of the motivation behind this partnership was undergirded by the reality that both communities share the same city, and while we didn't agree on issues of faith and divinity, we believed we could work for the good of the city we called home. One of the exercises we did was come up with ten questions for each community—e.g., why would a loving God allow such horrible suffering and such evil in our world? Or, if there is not a higher power, consciousness, or being, how do we even know what evil is? And so on. I'm sure many of the leaders of these different communities rolled their eyes at these questions, but these were the questions that members of our congregations or associations were asking, and each community—atheist and Christian—wanted to do their best to answer these ten questions with intellectual integrity without insulting the other. I taught several of the sessions for our church, but the one I taught that latched on to me and ended up opening up the gateway that lead to the journey of undoing included a statement made by famed atheist Richard Dawkins. In a video clip I showed to the west campus of our church, Dawkins said something to the following: I don't believe Christians believe in God, I believe they believe in their belief in God. He went on and showed proof for this by giving overwhelming examples—our treatment of other religions, the environment, along with our treatment of money. His insinuation was that if we truly believed in the God of the Bible, we Christians could not justify the way we live. His point was convicting: we have created projections of a God, or a belief system, that look more like deified versions of ourselves. We have, in essence, made our belief system into the God we worship. I showed this short video to my audience assuming it would make a deep impact on them, assuming that I, the pastor, was immune to the shallow Christianity that Dawkins was essentially attacking. But I wasn't. That little thought, planted deeply in my subconscious, became the undoing of this pastor. I assume Dawkins would be proud and disappointed at the same time. Proud because it did lead me to believe that my god was not the God of all creation, but a belief system about God, a system that is still being dismantled. Disappointed because it did not ultimately lead me to disbelief, but rather into a much fuller faith through the journey of undoing.

Part 2 of the book is sort of a "where do we go from here?" When a person, at a very existential level, is undone, a recreating, has to take place or they are left in the rubble of yesterday. Undoing brings about a sort of trauma—for me it resulted in high levels of anxiety and depression, which I will both talk about and show examples of later on in the book. To rise from this undoing, resilience is required. This is the subject of part 2 in this book, resilience theory and how I applied it to my life.

Acknowledgments

I would like to take a moment and acknowledge a few people: I want to thank Alex Shootman, Jeff Sandefer, and Dennis Jeffery, who encouraged me to move through this. It is said the only way to deal with the deep needs of the soul is not to go around or above or underneath the problem, but through it. You all gave me permission to take the time I needed to do the hard, interior work. I also thank the staff and my professors at Portland Seminary for not only challenging me academically, but for creating an environment for me to grow and heal, and the permission to see differently.

Thank you to Austin New Church for becoming more than a dream, for being a people who were crazy enough to believe the church could be something different than we all had experienced in the past. Thank you to my friend and co-pastor Austin Evers and the elders of Church at East for your patience, leadership, and grace, for being the church we all imagined in our hearts, and for allowing one of your pastors to leave because he needed the space for growth and healing. I love you all!

Thank you to my core friends and roommates at Portland Seminary, Savoy (who selflessly edited the first version of this manuscript), Sarah, Mel, Seth, Blair, and Jenn. You each played a very important role in this process. Our talks were challenging and insightful, but most of all, you all embodied the essence of true friendship, and you gave me the physical and emotional space I needed to take this journey. Portland will always be special because of you.

Most of all, thank you to my family. My kids, Serena, Ashton, Eden, and Elie, who will hopefully read this later in life, and who will all one day, by the grace of God, face midlife, but will hopefully handle it way better than I did. You showed grace to me in ways I can't fathom. You stuck by me in ways that still surprise me, and if it is even possible, your commitment to me was a guiding angel in my life. Sarah, thank you isn't enough. It does not encompass the way I feel for you. You lead and lead well. You wore a mantle that was supposed to be carried by both of us. You gave insight and wisdom when I had none. But most of all you loved and loved well. You loved to the point of your own depletion. You, my love, have been the best example of Christ that I have ever experienced. Thank you for being you!

Part 1: **The Undoing**

Introduction

The book you hold in your hand is part memoir, part pastoral advice, and part companion. It is a memoir because it is the story of my life up to this point. It is an attempt at pulling back the curtain to expose the truth and brokenness exacerbated by drivenness in my personal life. A drivenness that has been played out most in my pastoral roles. I am or was, by trade and academic training, a pastor. I write this book primarily from the perspective of a pastor. From the perspective of a pastor who has experienced much success and yet ended up with a diagnosis of high-functioning depression with PTSD symptoms. While I write this primarily from the perspective of a pastor, it is more generally from the perspective of a leader groomed within the construct of the American dream. I write this because I have learned this is not unique to me. Rather, the very depression and burnout I experienced is felt by an ever-growing number of leaders and pastors today. I have pastored three churches, and played an interim role at two other churches, in order to help them transition to new leadership and grow through rough times within the different congregations. I have planted three churches, two of which are still doing well. This is the context through which I write. This book is the revealing of my own personal darkness and brokenness that has for so long been covered up and denied by my profession and internal need to prove that I could indeed accomplish all I set out to accomplish. It is a story about a man who was driven by the negative rather than the positive, by who he didn't want to become rather than who he desired to be. It is a story of a man who, despite all his drivenness, had all of his expectations frustrated, and yet through that found a better way. A man whose desires were withered into nothingness, which resulted in deep peace. A man who is strong both in stature and tone, but didn't know true strength until he was brought to the place of weakness. It was at these places of nothingness, frustration, and weakness that I learned to live again.

Why is my memoir important for you? I'm not a celebrity. This is true. But I am not a celebrity on purpose. I fought the celebrity culture of the church to the best of my ability . . . and I lost. In place of a personal Instagram account, which allowed me to platform my personal "greatness" (in humility of course), I have a family account. In place of a personal website, FirstNameLastName.com, I have a website that platforms my family as we journey through life. When asked to do national conferences in the past, I said no (a classic example of what it means to "cut off your nose to spite your face."). I used to tell myself this was noble, that the celebrity culture within the church world was disgusting (I still believe this), and my way to fight it was to react against it. I was very caustic and angry about it. I saw the lies and deceit that swirled around it. I experienced the abdication of personal pastoral roles for the promise of national notoriety that demanded fabrication on many fronts to keep the platform healthy. In fact, I wholeheartedly stand with James Hunter when he says the way of true Christ-oriented leadership is the "antithesis of celebrity."[1] He goes on to say:

> [Christian] Celebrity is, in effect, based on an inflated brilliance, accomplishment, or spirituality generated and perpetuated by publicity. It is an artifice and, therefore, a type of fraud . . . Celebrity must, of necessity, draw attention to itself.[2]

There is nothing about the above statements that I disagree with. I believe celebrity in the Christian leadership realm to be a disease within the church. However, to agree with it wasn't enough. To live in the negative is to constantly seek out deconstruction. Deconstruction is only half of the whole. If one allows themselves to solely function in deconstruction, they become, by their very nature, destructive. We are not compartmentalized beings. If we do not move from deconstruction to reconstruction, then our proclivity for deconstruction will slowly devolve into a weapon aimed at destroying everything else in our lives, even the relationships we love. I allowed myself to believe that the remedy to this celebrity curse was to allow my life to be driven by the negative—what "not to be" rather than the positive side of who I was supposed to be. Rather than becoming a faithful presence in the world I was living, I wanted to destroy what I believed to be destroying others. Sounds noble on the surface, but it's self-destructive. When one is motivated by who not to be rather than who one is, joy is never a reality. Maybe this is

1. Hunter, *To Change the World*, 260.
2. Hunter, *To Change the World*, 260.

what caused my anger to be that much more ignited. I couldn't stand the fact that all of these folks who were posturing their platform to be a celebrity also seemed to be experiencing joy. It wasn't enough for me to live out my values in the midst of a celebrity culture; I wanted to fight it so that those benefiting from the system would feel as miserable as I was, and I, in some sick way, believed their misery would bring me joy. Of course, I would have never said that, but often times it's not till we have climbed out of the dark hole and are looking down that we can see clearly. The truth is, I believed a dismantling of the celebrity system would vindicate my fight. There's the irony. I wanted a mass population to vindicate me. In other words, I wanted what they had, just for a different reason. I wanted to become the anti-celebrity celebrity. This is often what happens when that which we know to be true in our hearts attempts to coexist with the lies we lust after. This is the internal fork in the road. We have to choose one or the other. I am a huge proponent of third-way thinking. Both/and. In this case I was trying to justify a philosophical schizophrenia, and schizophrenia is never healthy. I don't know why I believed that I needed to be driven by the negative or be a crusader against something, rather than simply live my life for something better. Maybe it is the crusader and war metaphors that plague Western Christianity, or maybe I was just afraid if I didn't fight and thus defeat something, I would end up becoming it. In some twisted way I believed I was sent by God to slowly disarm this monster of popularity and celebrity in the church. For some reason I thought this was something I could do. What I couldn't see was that maybe, just maybe, I should trust the same God who was developing me to also mold these very folks who found themselves in the ranks of celebrity. Maybe God was at work in them just as he was at work in me, if not more. Maybe God was doing something through them, and at the same time changing them, just as he was moving through me while simultaneously convicting me of my darkness. I wonder what things would have been like if I would have simply focused on living out my truth and belief about the church. I wonder how many relationships could have been saved. This is both the beauty and curse of hindsight. The truth is, being motivated by the negative has plagued me since I was very young.

At the young age of ten, eleven, twelve—I don't remember exactly—I was overweight. I hated that I was overweight, but at that point in my life hatred for a thing didn't drive me as much as my love for cake. But then I had an epiphany. I was thirteen, that I remember. I was spending a day with my family in a mall in Tulsa, Oklahoma. We were on the upper level of the mall, walking by the food court, when I heard a young boy yell out to his dad, "Come on Dad, hurry, I want to show you something." To this day, I can't figure out why this loud obnoxious request by this little boy grabbed my attention. We've all been in malls before, these temples of consumerism—they are loud, people are yelling, kids are constantly asking their parents for more stuff, and yet for some reason it was like the entire mall grew silent except for this one request yelled at a father who for some reason wasn't obeying the demands of his son. So, I turned around to see who this father was, and there he was, a very overweight man, in clothes too small, sweating and unable to keep up with his son. Right then and there, I determined that was not going to be me. I was going to be a father that would not only keep up with his kids, but would be teasing them about keeping up with him. I've been working out ever since, and my kids do, indeed, have a hard time keeping up with me. It was the fear or hatred of an inability to control my own food intake which might drive me to become less than my ideal of a healthy man that kept me moving for so long. I guess that's where it started for me, being driven by the negative. It paid off. My results were amazing. I was driven to have the best body I could have and be in the best shape I could be in. Within a couple years I had gone from an overweight thirteen-year-old to a person obsessed with fitness. At first, like all areas of life, my drivenness seemed to yield amazing results, but as time went on, and as I began to climb into my thirties, that same drivenness became destructive. Here I am in my early forties, and I have suffered multiple herniated discs, a cracked sternum, torn rotator cuffs, a torn pec, and many other smaller injuries. By the time I was in my early thirties, my negative motivations (who I didn't want to be) morphed into the motivation of vanity, which is typically how this whole thing progresses. Until someone said something so simple to me: "What if you quit training for vain reasons—a well-built body and impressive strength—and started training for a healthier you? Set fun goals, and train for them." It was so simple yet had been so elusive to me. My whole point being, I allowed the negative to motivate me rather than the positive, and while the negative earned me more immediate results, in the end it has cost me a very beat-up body.

I was eighteen years old when my parents divorced. As one can imagine, this derailed any immediate vision of college or the normal life a teenager desires to live. It did, however, open my eyes to the kind of man I didn't want to be. This is a weird one to write about. I love my father, and since the divorce, we have a good relationship. My dad is a good man. So, allow me to say that. But at that time, in that moment in my history, I was filled with anger and hatred yet again. Much like the impact of the overweight man in the story above, I decided that I was not going to be the kind of man that forced brokenness on his family.

It wasn't just my dad. There was my grandfather, my mom's dad, who was a wonderful grandfather. As I grew older, we grew apart relationally, for immature reasons on both sides. I didn't grow up around that side of the family, and consequently I viewed life differently than he did. And I was, even at a young age, willing to question conventional wisdom and ways of doing things, and my grandfather didn't know what to do with that. At the same time, my grandfather was, as I saw it back then, stuck in his ways. Unwilling to grow and explore the world. Uninterested in seeing the world differently. And I had no space to respect a man like that. The truth is, I was a young, prideful kid who had no intention of respecting the traditions my grandfather had come to own as ultimate truth. His inability to make room for me to grow as an individual and my lack of respect for his way of seeing the world caused for later conflict. This man, my grandfather, did what any good grandfather would do in the midst of a divorce: he tried to step in and become that father figure he assumed I needed. But I didn't need it, or maybe I didn't want it. At least not from him, because, like my father at that time, my grandfather was not the kind of man I wanted to become. So when people, in paying me a compliment, would say things like, "You remind me of your grandfather when you do that" or "That's just like your dad, he was so good at . . . ," it made me angrier. I didn't know how to see the good coexisting with what I knew to be negative. I allowed the anger to fill me so full that I saw the world through dualistic eyes—good or bad, all or nothing.

If I had some of the good qualities of my dad and grandfather, then I surely had some of the negative. So, at the age of eighteen, I began to once again allow the negative to direct and guide me. Rather than allowing myself to paint a picture of the type of man I wanted to be and then empowering myself to live into that, all the while recognizing the truth that much of who I wanted to be actually required many of the positive qualities embodied by both my father and grandfather.

I am, what I consider, an avid reader. I haven't always been one; in fact, I don't think I read my first full book until I was twenty-one. I know, the immediate question beginning to fly around is, "How did you do those book reports in school?" Well, I'm not sure of the statute of limitations on junior high or high school grades, so I'll just plead the fifth. Speaking of school,

I was one of those students, and my parents can vouch for this, that was a straight-C student. It's not because I didn't study. I did. I studied a lot. More so than my brother and friends who were straight-A students. I don't know what it was or why, but when it came to taking tests, it didn't seem to matter how much I had studied . . . well, it did, because all the studying I did saved me from Fs, but never yielded better than Cs. The one thing school did for me was make me feel stupid. I had great teachers. I admired them. But in school one's worth was equal to one's grades, and I couldn't ever figure out how to bring my grades up. Since then, I've learned and studied on subjects such as memory, learning styles, and different pedagogical systems, and it would seem I'm not cut out for a typical school setting. This would only prove true when I attempted college in Pensacola, Florida. Again, I had to study late nights to pull off a C average. Traditional classroom education, from what I knew, was not for me. Then something changed. That powerful monster of negativity found a way to raise its head and drive me again. It was the Christmas after my Sarah, and I were married. I was twenty-four and her grandfather and uncle were standing in the living room chatting about Christianity. I thought to myself, "I've read a few books on the subject, I grew up in a Christian home, and graduated from a one of those two-year mission schools, this is a conversation I can join." I. Was. Wrong. The depth to which they were speaking about Christology only reminded me of how much I didn't know. There was that old high school feeling again, "Dude, you're stupid." Before we left that evening, I asked Sarah's grandfather if I could borrow the books they had been discussing earlier. He graciously handed them over to me, and with the same negative determination to never feel stupid again, I began my journey to becoming an avid reader. I consumed reading like it was going out of style. There's a lot of good that came from this one. I did, indeed, learn a lot. I learned how to learn. In fact, learning became exciting to me. Books were the door to new philosophical and academic levels that I didn't know existed. But, since I was driven by the negative—"not to be stupid"—rather than the positive—"exploring and learning new worlds and ideas while strengthening my imagination and creativity"—like the fitness example above, what had started as motivation via the negative had mutated into a drivenness motivated by vanity, and I allowed my new ability to learn and know to be wielded like a superpower. I could use knowledge to control and manipulate. Knowledge brought a newfound respect from others. In fact, after years of humble advice and guidance from very patient men and women, I would have to say achieving my MDiv from Portland Seminary and the writing of this book are the first two milestones in the world of academia and knowledge that have been motivated by a positive vision of who I desire to be.

There are several more examples I could write about as to how I had allowed being driven by the negative to move me through life, but I think these few examples reveal a pattern in my life that was pretty well set. After all, this is not a memoir of my whole life, but it is my journey from a person who allowed himself to be formed and moved by the negative into a man who is now living and creating life based on a vision of beauty and truth. The only way to get from the negative to the positive is through. You don't get to go around. You do not get to dig beneath or jump over, you must go through it, and as this book will reveal, it is the through that is very dark.

So, while this book is indeed a memoir of sorts, it is also pastoral. When I began to go through what you will read in the book, I was being coached by Dan Steigerwald. Dan very much played an anchor in my life during this portion of my journey, where I felt as if I were in constant danger of drifting away. My many conversations with Dan acted as a tool of re-centering. They always brought me back to the place I needed to be in order to move onward. In fact, at one point, my family and I were about to take off on my three-month sabbatical with a two-month road trip throughout the Western US, and Dan began to speak to me about this growing epidemic of depression, burnout, and anxiety within the ranks of US pastors. At that time, I was shocked. I truly believed this was unique to me. I think, to some extent, this is why anxiety and depression end up taking such devastating tolls on those we love—silence. How could this be a growing epidemic, and at the same time I knew nothing about it? As Dan and I continued the conversation and I began to research much of what he was saying, I came to learn that, indeed, I was simply another fish in a large sea of pastoral burnout. The numbers were astonishing. In a world where we (the pastors) preach about ideas of sabbath and community, over 70 percent of pastors state they do not have a close friend, while over 50 percent leave full-time ministry after five years due to burnout and exhaustion.[3] These are not the only staggering statistics, but it seems the simple remedy to much of this is for pastors to engage in regular spiritual renewal practices, sabbath rhythms, and connecting to truly supportive people.[4] Ironically, these are the very things we attempt to pastor our people into. We know,

3. Meek eta al., "Maintaining Personal Resiliency.".
4. Chandler, "Pastoral Burnout."

on the surface, that our people need these structures within their life to live out the joy and love of Christ, but for some reason it appears we don't practice what we preach. Maybe we think we are exempt from these personal needs because we work for God. Maybe we, like many others, work in a church world that models the secular business model with jobs based on measurables such as numbers and income, and we know if we don't deliver, our livelihood is on the line. Thus, we use the spiritual language to cover up our secular drive. We begin to tell ourselves that we will begin to embrace these structures of rest and renewal once we secure a certain number of members and giving. We all know that number never seems to be enough. But whatever the reason, we excuse ourselves from the need of external pastoral care, structures of rest and renewal, and I am now one of the statistics of this all-too-regular burnout that has been, for some reason, silenced. This is where the pastoral role of this book comes in. Maybe you, the reader, are in the middle of this. Maybe you are now, like me, one of the statistics, and are wondering, "Now what?" Maybe you are on the verge of what I will write about in the following pages. Maybe you are right in the middle of something similar to the story I tell. Or maybe you know or are married to someone who is going through this. I hope and pray this book helps guide you through and beyond your current state. It cannot be completely pastoral, because it is not a person to be in relationship with, but I do pray it is a pastoral voice of grace and wisdom as you move from where you are to where you are destined to be.

Finally, I have written this book to be a companion in your journey. The two statistics I mention above and the few mentioned in chapter 1 reveals to us that much of the reason people do not reinvent themselves, make it through to the other side, or develop resilience during and after times of liminality is a result of loneliness. As stated above, I was a bit shocked to find out that this seemed to be an epidemic rather than my own personal isolated bout with depression and burnout. I am convinced to this day, had it not been for my professors and friends at Portland Seminary and my family, I would not have made it through this. There seem to be many pathways to success, and rarely a one-size-fits-all equation, but the one way to assure failure is to go it alone. If you are one who boasts of rarely asking for help, then, my friend, you are thin ice. You need companions. Like the pastoral role of this book, the companion value is not complete. You need flesh-and-blood companions, you need to hear actual voices, most of all you need to be surrounded by folks you can talk with. This book can't provide that, but it can remind you that you are not alone, that there are others who have been through what you are going through, or what the person you know is going through. This book, while not a substitute for actual people you need in your life, is, another voice. A voice you will be able to relate to. A voice that gives permission to admit the things you are feeling no matter how dark they may seem. A voice that says, "Let's go. You can do this. I've been there."

Questions

In the last chapter of this book I lay out a tool for you to use as you move forward in life. Before I define the tool, and how I use it in my own life, I ask a question about vision. Vision for your life. Nothing elaborate, rather something simple. Don't worry about answering that question now, you'll get there soon enough. I do, however, have a few other questions that I believe you should begin to think about as you begin to read this book. They may seem irrelevant at first, but they are not. They are much like sun glasses as you walk toward the sun. They will have helped you see more clearly. Not unlike the seemingly irrelevant exercises Mr. Miyagi demands of Daniel in the 1984 movie *The Karate Kid*, these questions and your engagement with them will begin to develop a sort of subconscious strength that will begin to be more obvious as we begin to think in the way of vocational vision in relation to your life. If you can't answer these questions, your vision may end up being a quick answer, or an answer imposed on you from your culture, upbringing, past (failures or accomplishments), or something superficial, like "I want see a thousand souls saved" or "I see myself leading the new world order"—okay, probably not that extreme, but you get my point.

After decades of being in leadership roles, I have to admit the whole leadership/vision conversation brings out the cynic in me, for reasons unnecessary to discuss at this time. My point is this: no matter your view on leadership, if you can't lead yourself, it doesn't matter. Period. And while this is not a leadership book, I believe one of the subsequent results of developing personal resilience through times of depression, burnout, and lostness is the development of personal leadership. You will learn to lead you! So, come back to these questions as you read this book. These questions will come into play and prove important as you set up your own way forward and develop personal resilience.

Question 1: What makes you come alive? Seriously. That's it. What do you love to do? Don't list out ten or twenty things. Narrow it down. Think back over your life, even if you have made career choices or relationship choices that have left you burned out and dry. Have there been times when you felt fully alive? If so, what were you doing? I'm not talking about big elaborate conquests. In fact, I'm not talking about accomplishments. I'm not talking about the feeling you get when you are praised by other people. I'm talking about the three or four things you do that make you feel alive not matter who sees or compliments you. For me, one is public speaking. I love it. I do. I don't need anyone to approach me after one of my talks to compliment me, or inform me of how blessed they are or how challenged they are to make me feel alive. Don't get me wrong, compliments are nice, but the art of public speaking is one of the actions that really make me feel alive. Coming in at a close second, third, and fourth place are playing with my family, fitness, and adventure. So, as I was going through my own personal development of resilience, I had to create space and pathways that allowed me to engage these elements that brought life to me. You will too.

Question 2: What gives you the deepest sense of peace? Through times of anxiety, depression, and burnout our minds often mirror the devil's playground. Full of chaos, haunting images, and fears about a tomorrow that has not yet arrived. You need to find your peace, and once you know what and/or where that is, you need to figure out how to return there often. This could be nature. It could be a quiet morning. It may be long runs. Whatever it is, or wherever it is, give yourself permission, especially when you are overwhelmed, to hit pause on what you are doing and find that place of peace. To take it a step further, it is a real bonus when that which makes you feel truly alive can overlap with that which brings you deep peace.

Question 3: Who has it worse than you? I know, that sounds awful. But hang with me. This is not about judgment, this is about getting out of and over yourself. When we are fixated on the real problems going on inside of us, as large as those problems actually are, we figure out how to magnify them if we keep ourselves isolated. In much of the self-help cult of the day, I hear many folks say something to the effect of, "Once I get better . . ." or "Once I am well . . ." or "Once I fix myself, then I will begin to serve others." This type of thinking only leads to a sort of negative self-absorption that keeps us spinning around the same drain for years. Getting outside of yourself and asking "Who has it worse than me?" allows for perspective, on both our world and our actual problems. Make space and take time to both engage and serve those who have it worse than you. These actions remind us that we can make a difference, that life isn't over, and maybe most of all, it allows us to get out of the way of our own healing and allows the spirit to work in us in a very healing way while we work in a healing way toward those who actually "have it worse than us." Please hear me, you won't feel like doing this. And that is part of the genius of it—acting against your distorted feelings to do what you know you should do, for those who need it. As a recommended exercise, I would suggest that after you engage and serve the person or population who "has it worse than you," take some intentional reflective time at the end of your service and write in a journal. Write about your feelings. Write about your interaction. Write about details you noticed about those you served. Then wrap it up by saying a short prayer for them. Not you. Them. "Wax on, Wax off."

Let's Go!

So here we go. You are equipped with the three questions: What makes you come alive? What brings you peace? And who has it worse than you? Keep these questions in front of you as you move through this book.

Chapter 1: **Disillusioned**

Be still: There is no longer any need of comment. It was a lucky wind that blew away his halo with his cares, a lucky sea that drowned his reputation.

—THOMAS MERTON

In all the mad incongruity, the turgid stultiloquy of life, I felt, at least, securely anchored to myself. Whatever the vacillations of other people, I thought myself terrifically constant. But now, here I am, dragging a frayed line, and my anchor gone.

—JOHN STEINBECK

I have decided to remove the veil from the beginning of the book. One of the practices I stepped up during this period of undoing was journaling. I needed a way to simply say what I was feeling without scaring those around me. For more than a decade I have had a stage presence. There is nothing wrong with this, in fact, I love it. I feel as if my stage presence was, for the most part, transparent. However, as a public speaker, one's main goal is to draw people in to listen to the message you hope will transform them. Part of the crafting work one does is polishing the transparency. For instance, as a public speaker I can say, "I have been struggling with lust." I can't say, "I have been lusting over so-and-so's breasts." Why? Because the point of my talk is not that of confession. If all I wanted to do was confess to people, then great, that may be different. But when I talk, I typically have a point bigger than my confession. Admitting to a desire to do drugs, or have sex with someone else, or harm a specific person may offend someone in the audience so greatly that they never hear my actual point. As a speaker,

I have failed. So, in order to get to the point, one simply cleans up their transparency.

I am a firm believer that everyone needs to get the thoughts and struggles they are dealing with out of their system without a filter. For some that may be going on a walk and speaking out loud. For others that may be in a group or individual therapy session or a confessional booth to a priest. And still others may find release in writing down their thoughts. For me it was my journal. I had a few friends I confided in with unfiltered confession, but for the most part it was my journal. Since then, I have deleted most of the stuff I had written. I'm not advising this. Maybe you need to keep your journals. I just didn't feel I needed to keep all of them. However, I did keep some of them, and I have included a collage of those entries in this chapter. They are dark. They are obscene. They are offensive. But they are honest. It is how I felt. I know, I seem to be going against the very principle I just defended about polishing my transparency. I get that. However, this time my unfiltered thoughts are actually part of my point. Since I've gone through this, I have come to the realization that I am not a minority. Many others are facing and dealing with the exact same mental games I reveal in my journal entries, yet many others never get the help they need because they are so ashamed of the very thoughts that have haunted their minds. They don't want to admit they have had these sorts of thoughts and feelings. So, they tuck them away and deny it. I wanted to do the opposite. I wanted to use some of my own journal entries to reveal how far down I had fallen, to say you are not alone. So, as a final warning, there is a decent amount of cursing. There are dark thoughts, and if these things are offensive to you, please skip to page 18 under the heading "Recalling," and just know, after twelve years of ministry and being a very public figure, I crashed and crashed hard. I came to a very dark place and was diagnosed with high-functioning depression. However, if you, like me, have been to these dark places, and feel shame for the thoughts of anger or despair you have entertained, please read on, and simply know you are not alone. When I was writing in my journal, I was writing in the way of a confession, as if I were sitting next to God or a friend and recalling the last several years.

WARNING: Journal Collage

Fuck! How the fuck did I get here? I packed up my whole family and drove them from the only city we've known as home to a small town in the middle of the cornfields with a population smaller than my personal network. Insane? Desperate? I'm not sure. A friend of mine writes in one of his songs, "maybe I go because I'm chasing something . . . maybe I go because something is chasing me."[1] If I ran because something was chasing me, then it followed me here.

So, how the fuck did I get here within myself? I feel more lost than ever. Faith crisis is an understatement. The faith tradition I come from claims that the satan or the enemy is the author of this confusion. If that is true then God has vacated, if he was ever here in the first place, my head, and this enemy, this satan, has taken up its writing career between my ears. I can't differentiate between the past and the present and can't see far enough ahead of now to hope for a future.

My insecurities overshadow me like a slavemaster. The voices in my head are louder than any other voice of reason that may attempt to speak up. Shadows haunt me as if they were predators and I their prey. Words and sentiments that I used and heard so fondly are now curses to my soul. I'm so tired of trying to be everyone's fucking rock. I have no authority to call off the shadows. They show up whenever they feel like it. They control their own presence.

Mentally and emotionally I feel as if I have crossed a threshold that scares the shit out of me. It is so hard to find a peaceful place, and it makes no sense. I have four amazing kids! I have a wonderful and faithful wife, and an amazing extended family. I have all these things going for me, and all I fantasize over escape and death. Taking measures that one does not come back from. What the fuck is that about? Ironically, I am afraid of death, apparently that is odd for a pastor. I just want the images in my head to stop. I've prayed. I've written. I've confessed. I've argued with myself, and nothing. My head is a minefield, and I can't get out of it. People tell me, I need a therapist or a psychologist—I need a fucking exorcist to cast out the demons in my head. I have too many things going for me, yet I find myself regretting mistakes I didn't make. I find myself wanting to do horrible things, just to feel them.

A year ago we celebrated our fifteenth anniversary, with a couple hundred of our friends. Now, I'm a stranger in a strange land. The sick humor behind all of this, is that it was chosen. So, I don't really have room to complain. According to Campbell, I'm probably not crazy, rather I'm in the "abyss" portion of the hero's journey. At least that's the shit I'm

1. David Ramirez, "Stick Around," *Apologies* (2012).

telling myself. Who knows, I sure as hell don't feel like a hero, much less a healthy human, at best I feel like two persons within one body fighting each other for control of the central mood and thought of the day.

I'm not sure when it all started or how far back it goes. What I know is that it was a gradual descent into this abyss of lostness. This is not where pastoring is supposed to lead. This is not how a "servant of God" is supposed to end up. We are supposed to be the ones who understand, at least, to some extent, what God is doing or has been doing. We are not the ones who are supposed to feel like we've had the wool pulled over our eyes. I can't tell if I'm waking up from being disillusioned or I have become disillusioned or maybe both.

Shit, we didn't even want to get into this whole church thing. Our life together started with one common thought, "We love God but not the church, so we're going to stay away from the church," and here we are sixteen years later as casualties of it—burned out, depressed church planters escaping the residual stress of the city and church world. I'm such a cliche. What the fuck happened? Why didn't we jump off this train when we knew we were supposed to? Did we know we were supposed to? Did we have any idea that disillusionment would be the dead end we ran into? Were we supposed to know? The idea behind the word "disillusioned" is to be disappointed in someone or something that one discovers to be less good than one had believed. Is God less good than I believed he was? I feel like I'm so far gone that I couldn't even begin to parse out, identify, or assign the "someone" or "something" to one person or one event or institution or even if I should, but "disillusioned" seems to be the word that keeps coming to the forefront of defining how I feel or felt or am feeling.

Since leaving the church world, I haven't been able to commit to a local body. I can't hear anything without thinking it is bullshit, and I can't hear a sermon without being overcritical of the pastor's style, her hermeneutical approach, or fluffed-up personal stories—there I go again.

My fuse is shorter than my memory, and I have a hard time imagining something different. This used to be a strength of mine—I've always been good at imagining new horizons and possibilities, but now I have a hard time imagining anything positive at all. My left eye ticks. I can't seem to trust anyone, and I don't know what or who or even if I believe anymore. I know I'm angry at God, but not the angry that is very much en vogue with younger Christians. I'm pretty pissed off at him, or it, or her right now. I just don't like this God thing. There are certain songs I will hear, that used to cause me to fall into a euphoric state, that now cause internal rage. The other day a friend of mine told me that I may have to tread deeper into the waters that anger and scare me before I can get through them. But I don't think I trust God with those waters. I tried that earlier during this period and God let me fall hard and it hurt, and I'm not willing to go through that again. My friend says I have to be. I have to be willing to go there with God. But I don't think I can. I don't think I can let this God hurt me or abandon me in the places I most fear again with the ones I most love.

I'm rambling, back to where I am. This three-month sabbatical has now been going on for nine months. The longer I am off the less I want to come back, which scares me. The more I am supposed to be healing the angrier I become. The more I am supposed to get in tune with God the less I want to be around him. The more I attempt to be an agent of redemption, the more I seem punished for it. At some level I feel, no, I can confidently say, I know I'm evolving into a new person, however at another level, I am being undone in a very scary way. It doesn't fit into the way I understand God. But it's where I am, and I don't really have a category for it. I think some people would say I have reached the point of unbelief. Maybe, but I don't think the lack of categories equates to the lack of belief. Maybe I'm coming to the realization that I didn't so much believe in the real God as much as I believed in belief in this God or a deified projection of myself. I know I'm not falling into atheism. I've tried that venture one too many times and God or logic or experience, or all three, hasn't let that work for me. But I don't really have a category to define where I am.

Recalling

Where did all of this begin? When did I begin down this road of undoing? The best I can recall is about five years ago we had come home from a church event and we were standing in our kitchen, and looked at each other from across the room and one of us said, "I just want to fall off the map. Something's not right with this whole thing." The reason I can't remember who said this is because we shared the exact same feelings and this confession could have come just as easily from the one as it could have the other. We just didn't know how to identify it. We didn't know where to go or what to do. But that's as far back as I can recall, at least, that's the moment that stands out in my head. I know I made a lot of choices based on my nature of taking responsibility for things that I should have allowed to fall apart. I don't know if that comes from being a first-born, or being a first-born from a divorced family. Whatever it is, I put more pressure on myself than those around me do. And it can get ugly. Even though we knew we were to fall off the map, we never did. Like most of life, some things got better but others not so much. I found that in order for us to function in our personal context, the best way forward was for me to lean harder into the false self. Not in an obvious way. I didn't have an epiphany to metaphorically bury myself, but I knew in order to continue down this same road at our capacity, being me wasn't going to work. Still not sure why I thought that was a viable option for life. Except this was a coping mechanism I learned a long time ago to be who my family needed me to be through some early hard times.

I do remember talking with a friend of mine, also a former pastor, about remaining true to oneself while having to wear so many hats and keeping all the plates in the air. I asked him, "How do you do it? How do you wear all the hats we wear and stay or, at least, appear joyful in life?" My question turned into a confession: "I feel like I'm lost, like I'm good at nothing. I'm busy picking up the slack to keep things going, I wear too many hats and never have the opportunity to focus on one thing." I recognize this is acedia, not according to Webster, but according to the way ancient monks defined it. I had the power to change things, I just didn't, I hid behind my busyness to avoid the hard work of changing the reality I had constructed. By this time, I was lost in my own world. He continued by saying, "I'm learning to be me in every scenario. That way, I'm always being true to who God made me to be, and when one does that, the focus shifts. It's not about how many hats you wear, it's about being the same person under each hat." Such wisdom, and yet so difficult. He was right, but I felt too lost to find my way there.

I guess it was about four years ago I began to experience some severe anxiety—at one point, the anxiety was so strong that my brain had to reset—I was walking through my bedroom and I passed out. I was so desperate and began to tread into the waters of transparency or grasping at straws. Either way, I wanted to be free. I put it out there to my coworkers but it mostly fell on deaf ears—after all, I was the tough, get-it-done person with the hard exterior. Another local pastor, who had, a year before, experienced the same thing and was also diagnosed with high-functioning depression took the time to speak truth to me. He gave me his time and assisted me in being truthful by naming issues for what they were. Another colleague I worked with would reach out to make sure I was okay. My superintendent, who must have been very perceptive, or else I was wearing it on my sleeve, called me and offered counseling and a sabbatical. I took neither because of how busy I was. When I look back, I'm not sure I was too busy. My problem was that I was trying to function and be someone I wasn't. And it took its toll on us.

I still can't figure out where it all went wrong, but everything was wrong. Not wrong like morally wrong or some sort of obvious evil lurking around the corner kind of wrong, but wrong like missing the point wrong. That's it. We started out with this amazing vision. Our motivations were proper and good. The focus of life and faith was the true, the good, and the beautiful. However, somewhere along the line, we devolved into missing the point. All of our efforts were about intentionally missing the point, but we didn't realize it. It was an unintentional intentionality. We set out to be different, to be other than, in fact, we began to receive press, respect, and notoriety due to our otherness. But we weren't other. At least not truly other. We were other on a surface level but no more other than different kids at a Halloween party. Sure, my kid is dressed up like Dracula at the church Hallelujah night and Jeff's kid is dressed up like Bathsheba or a slutty nurse or a cross-dressing Jacob, never mind, what Jeff's kid dressed up like is not the point. The point is that my kid and his kid were dressed differently, yet at the end of the day both kids are wearing costumes that were supposed to cover their true identity. Everything was wrong like that. We had created a system and name that supported the costume, even though our costume was authenticity. To be other, we were simply regurgitating old solutions for modern dilemmas. Of course, it didn't seem that obvious because the old ideas were masked to look like new ideas, but they weren't new they were the same ideas in different costumes. In fact, they were surface adjustments without in-depth changes. Maybe this is always the result when we are convinced we have to be in control of the change, and we are afraid to allow natural evolution to take its course. I know the anxiety created from pretending we were something that we weren't was tearing me apart. I began to see everything through this lens. All the new Christian books coming out were the same damn thing in a different costume. Nothing was authentic anymore. In the words of the *Fight Club* narrator, "Nothing's real. Everything's far away. Everything's a copy of a copy of a copy."[2] Yet we were building our lives on the illusion that we were original. However, this was not the part that pushed me over the edge. It should have been, but it wasn't.

2. Palahniuk, *Fight Club*, 21.

The part that sent me over the edge was that we started to believe the deception as true. We started to defend it.

Distancing from the Pack

I found myself distancing myself from anything that was Christian. Wanting to answer the "So, what do you do?" question with anything other than "I'm a pastor." Because if this is what being a pastor was, I wanted nothing to do with it. This is not unlike a scenario presented in Aldous Huxley's *Ape and Essence*. In *Ape and Essence*, the protagonist finds himself contemplating his current situation through the lens of the question as to "why" Gandhi had been assassinated:

> The whole story [Gandhi's assassination] included an inconsistency, almost a betrayal. This man who believed only in people had got himself involved in the sub-human mass-madness of nationalism, in the would-be super-human, but actually diabolic, institutions of the nation state. He got himself involved in these things, imagining that he could mitigate the madness and convert what was satanic in the state to something like humanity. But nationalism and the politics of power had proved too much for him. It is not at the center, not from within the organization, that the saint can cure our regimented insanity; it is only from without, at the periphery. If he makes himself part of the machine, in which the collective madness is incarnated, one or the other of two things is bound to happen: either he remains himself, in which case the machine will use him as long as it can and, when he becomes unusable, reject or destroy him. Or he will be transformed into the likeness of the mechanism with and against which he works, and in this case we shall see Holy Inquisitions and alliances with any tyrant prepared to guarantee ecclesiastical privileges.[3]

I reread it and reread it. I had to underline it. And I couldn't get away from that paragraph. I am afraid it is hauntingly true about way too many things in our world. In fact, most of the conversations I've been around lately about social change, faith, outreach, poverty, and politics seem to be so relevant to this text. It gets too hard. We swap original prophetic imagination for success, platforms, and celebrity, all in the name of "change," but in the end, we are changed to the conventional undercurrent or used and spit out. We have not killed the monsters of old, we have only dressed them in new

3. Huxley, *Ape and Essence*, 8.

clothes. I was being spit out, and the institution and the God that I thought would rescue us from this seemed willing to protect this modern costume of an age-old illusion rather than unmask the facade.

Apparently, I'm not alone, but it does seem I am the very thing I sought to avoid. I am a statistic. This is more common than I thought. I personally have witnessed numerous pastors confess to being in a state of chronic fatigue. We are worn out on a daily and weekly basis. Upholding a facade for too long will do this to a person. I have listened to many pastors confess that their marriage is falling apart. Aren't our marriages supposed to be examples to the world rather than a mirror image? When life becomes a balancing act, something has to fall, and we live in a culture that says if anything takes the hit, it isn't the identity building career, it's the family. Depression also seems to be part of the norm. At the time of this writing, five pastors that I personally know have just been diagnosed with deep depression. Maybe depression is more prominent among the majority of personalities that make up the pastor population, or maybe living like a fake and failure forces one to a fork in the road—depression or buy in to the facade. All of these numbers seem to translate into a mass exodus from professional ministry for some and from the faith all together for others. In short, I feel like the very demon that has chased many of us out of the ministry or into a shell is the duality we have learned to live with. It is this duality that causes the crash. I wonder if the fact that I recognize that there is a duality is also a sign that somewhere the remedy has been growing in us all along, not unlike a slow groundswell. We have tried to live in both worlds, and it has driven us mad. The quest now is to find out how to starve the facade and breathe life into what we know to be the true, the good, and the beautiful.

Looking Ahead

I still very much wrestle with shadows. I don't know if they will ever die. There are still mornings I don't want to wake up and face the day. David Ramirez, has a song called "The Forgiven." In this song, he is talking about being a songwriter who desires to sing about truth. But he knows that it will affect his ticket sales. He has a few lines that read like this: "They love me for being honest, they love me for being myself, but the minute I mention Jesus, they want me to go to hell." He goes on and sings about the claims they make in order to demand he sings to the tune they desire: "You're just a songwriter, you ain't a preacher, we came to mourn you, not to look in the mirror. Sing about those hard times, sing about those women. We love the broken, not the forgiven."[4] In reality this is not that different from the way pastors have it.

When we "hire" a preacher, we want good, entertaining sermons that will motivate us to live more successful or moral daily lives. We want pastors we can look up to, rather than those who need to be pulled up. We want folks that seem to have it all together, and we even claim we want pastors who are transparent . . . until they are. Then we don't know what to do with it, nor how to deal with a man or woman who wrestles with the same things or worse than we do. Pastors know this. They know they have a show to perform, much like my singer-songwriter friend, and so we, the pastors, stuff it down and put on the show. Most of us are pretty good at it. We don't deal with it and the outcome is usually a masqueraded life or a fall from grace, in which we are never heard from again as we get swallowed up by our own brokenness.

I admit the collection of paragraphs from my journal entries are rough. The language I use is unwelcome in religious circles. Maybe it isn't unwelcome among the laity. It may very well be part of the secularized life of laity, but we certainly are uncomfortable with our pastors talking this way. I'm not sure why, maybe it humanizes us too much. I'm not advocating for cursing like it's a value of mine, but I do cuss. But even harder for us to swallow is not the cussing, but the descriptive depression I write about. The thoughts of running away, death, and unholy desires.

There have been plenty of stories in the past several years of pastors burning out, living secret lives that are uncovered and followed by great embarrassment and hurt. Typically, the response of the public, the same public that loved them at one point for putting on the show, lies somewhere between mockery to verbal and vocational execution for being broken. It shouldn't be this way. We pastors are flesh and blood, we struggle with darkness, depression, sadness, anger, and pain. We can't take more than others, so to speak. We are not less broken than the rest of those we serve, though we may be lonelier. Like the rest of those we serve, we are nothing more than forgiven folks on a journey towards God.

The pages that follow are not from a professional psychologist, nor someone who has figured it all out. As I said above, I still struggle. I am inviting you into a journey of confession and work. It was not easy for me to

4. David Ramirez, "The Forgiven," *The Rooster* (2013).

write some of these struggles. Some of them are very private and personal. However, as I began to uncover and meet pastors and leaders throughout different organizations and churches who have struggled in similar ways, I felt it best to at least do something with the pain and depression I had struggled with. I wanted to put it out there, for one, to say to those with the same struggle, "You're not alone in this." I also wanted to show you that even though my mind has been severely tormented and very dark at times, there is a way out, and the way out is not alone. Your way or the way for someone you love may be very different than mine. But we—and I say "we" because, while a struggle may be individual, the slow remedy will never be found in isolation—that is, my family, not I, came through this. My struggle affected my family, but my family surrounded me with love, patience, grace, and truth. They helped me shoulder this—for me, they are the heroes in the story because in a life that has been haunted by dark isolation in my head, they provided loving community within reality and offered me their hearts and souls as healing agents, and I was able to trust them with mine. This story is only a reality because of them. So, we invite you into this journey, to learn some of the things we learned, maybe to adapt some of the practices we implemented, and hopefully breathe some of the new beginnings that we are breathing.

While we write this for leaders and their families. We write this to all who find themselves living in the tension of what we long for and a darkness that continually haunts us. So, come with us down this path.

Chapter 2: What If It Doesn't Get Any Better than This?

"But in the end it's only a passing thing, this shadow; even darkness must pass."

—JRR TOLKIEN, *THE LORD OF THE RINGS*

"Above all, don't lie to yourself. The man who lies to himself and listens to his own lie comes to a point that he cannot distinguish the truth within him..."

—FYODOR DOSTOEVSKY, *THE BROTHERS KARAMAZOV*

Staring into oblivion as I sit idling in my driveway in my 2006 Honda Odyssey, which was already a hit on my pride, sense of autonomy, and self-image or facade, I'm not sure which, I was hit by a very sobering thought. The thought presented itself in the form of a question, but a question that seemed to have more notes of epiphany than it did randomness. The question was, "What if it doesn't get any better than this?" What?!?! That single question raged against every fiber of my being, every fiber that had been mended together by the American dream. After all, "better than this" is the underlying motivation behind the American dream. "If you work hard enough, it does get better than this!" The idea is that my American citizenship coupled with hard work guaranteed me some sort of "betterness" in life. But what if it didn't guarantee me this? What if it was never supposed to? And what was this betterness that my citizenship was supposed to guarantee? I had never asked that, I just assumed this betterness was something I wanted, and thus inherent in living according to the system of upward mobility. After all, I was a good white male American living in a suburban neighborhood, in a house with enough square feet to justify a house cleaner, respectable amount of debt, two vehicles, and a garnish of just enough pride to uphold our current lifestyle. Of course, this prefabricated betterness was something I wanted, even if I didn't know what it was. However, this little thought, "What if it doesn't get any better than this?," disrupted everything. It caused us to step off this conveyor belt and ask some fundamental question, the kind of questions that seemed so simple, yet so despised if you were a hard-working, good American.

In church there are some questions that are okay to ask: why is the carpet this color? Why did Jesus die for us? Did Jessie eat all the donuts again? But then there are some we are supposed to stay away from: How do we know Adam and Eve were even real humans, much less the first humans? Don't you think the Jonah story was more of a parable? When it comes to forgiveness, why does God expect me to do something he couldn't? These were the type of questions we were asking about our cultural acceptance: What was this betterness that we were supposed to trade our daily lives for? What if we don't want this betterness? What if we don't want the prefabricated American dream? What if we want to jump off the conveyor belt? Can we imagine a new kind of life that will seem foreign in our context? Jesus did say one can't serve two masters, which I translate to mean that we can't show equal allegiance to two entities. The tension within our lives was that we were living in a way that seemed to prove equal allegiance was possible. All of this was situated on an American Jesus, a Jesus who seemed to be in alignment with the American way and was in agreement with the betterness predicated on our American citizenship. In fact, it seemed Jesus was more American than we were. The more we began to ask these questions, the more it seemed we were not only being heretical in our religious commitments, but we were also being unpatriotic, as if the two were married to each other—a committed Christian, will always be a very good conservative American, in which dual allegiance is not only possible, but respectable and expected. Did we even think about it, or had we simply allowed the undercurrent to take us in the direction it was headed? Had we allowed the choice architects hidden within our religious, cultural, and social constructs to guide us into being part of a system that benefited them more than us?

"It" and "Better" Defined

"What if it doesn't get better than this?" The first task was to figure out what the "it" and "better" was. The better or more pointed question is, what did we assume life's telos to be? Where did we think we were headed in life? To what end were we traveling? The assumed answer to the question was: bigger, more, and security. By bigger we didn't necessarily mean quantity nor square feet, though each house we had purchased up to this point had been larger than the last, which of course necessitated more and nicer stuff to fill said houses and closets with more and nicer clothes. Each car had been nicer than the one before, which also meant more debt, accompanied by more prestige. Occupationally speaking, we were church planters and social entrepreneurs, and the church we were part of was growing, and the faster the church grew the better paid we were—without expounding any more, one can quickly see the poor motivation behind planned church growth. Of course, we like to use soul talk to disguise some of the underlying motivation, but nonetheless, larger church meant more work, and more work meant more busyness, and more busyness meant more stress, but all of this was supposed to lead to more notoriety and respect. To sustain the notoriety and respect we had to grow more in size, which resulted in the same cycle—more work, busyness, and stress. The cycle was endless, but the motivating factor was this idea or illusion or promise that we were building some sort of security we could rest in at some point in the future. Security was supposed to be the nest we would be able to rest in after a lifetime of achievements and accolades to show for all the work, stress, and busyness we sacrificed everything for, even our true self, in order to one day reap the benefit of all this sacrifice. While you may not be a pastor or even a religious leader, most of us can replace the occupation of "pastor" for another occupational label, but the ferris wheel is the same.

The "it" was life. What if "life" doesn't get better than this, better than the current cycle of growth, more work, stress, and busyness? Specifically, what if the church doesn't grow any larger? What if the next house isn't bigger? What if the next set of cars aren't better? What if our network stopped expanding? What if that security that we are aiming for actually protected us from the life we really longed for? Life was pretty good, and to be honest, on paper, most church planters would have loved our setup.

If I was living the life many of my counterparts were aiming for, then I had bought into a line of bullshit, bullshit that wasn't delivering what it was promising. I had put all my energies into the idea that one day life would go from ordinary to extraordinary. But what if it didn't? In fact, when I began to survey my own life and the lives of those living for the ethereal tomorrow when one day the extraordinary would materialize, what I realized was that tomorrow is always tomorrow, and the extraordinary that I was working toward existed on a sliding scale. As our life became bigger and more secure, the end goal grew in scope as well. We were never moving any closer to the end goal as expansion happened in our lives so did our desire for a larger end game, which demanded more expansion, which fed a continual growing lust for a larger nest to land in. In other words, I was never going to arrive. So, if it was never going to get better than this, is this the "it" we wanted to spend our lives living? The answer was a resounding "No!" No, it wasn't.

The True and False Self

To talk about what was going on or why it was happening in our souls, let's take a glimpse into the world of geography. Before we get there, I want to take a moment and talk about the false and true self, to add more weight to the geography metaphor.

Rather than attempting to write an entire chapter on these two ideas, I leave it to better authors than myself. There has been much publication about these two realities, not least by great thinkers such as Richard Rohr and the late Thomas Merton. For this section I will simply lean on Merton, from his work *New Seeds of Contemplation*.

Thomas Merton asserts that we have two warring identities: a false self and a true self. Whereas the true self is created and released through God-breathed activity, the false self results from energies committed to egocentric desires. From this place of egocentric desires, a self is constructed, portrayed, and positioned at the center of our world. When the false self assumes central position, it begins to exist under the assumption that all of reality revolves around and for the self and is thus ordered for personal glory.[1] All of the sudden, God looks like a deified version of me. Moral absolutes align with my moral perspectives, and since God looks a lot like me, my judgmental-projections upon others and reality are disguised as prophetic truths. These prophetic truths help me sustain the world I need to sustain that allows my false self to remain at the center and deserving of the praise received, thus solidifying the illusion I have created into objective reality. In other words,

---

1. Merton, *New Seeds of Contemplation*, 34.

the false self is an image predicated on the lie that my self-centered desires and the will of God for me are in alignment.

Many of us never succeed at becoming ourselves. We never actually become the particular God-ordained person we were intended to become. We never become the man, woman, artist, teacher, doctor, pastor, parent, or the spouse who is called for by all the circumstances and contexts of our individual lives, because we waste our years in vain effort to be some other woman, pastor, man, parent, doctor, artist, or spouse that we have been deceived into believing is better than who we are. For many absurd reasons, we become convinced that we are obligated to become somebody else who, like a dog on a leash, follows the call of conventional wisdom.

We wear out our bodies and minds in a hopeless endeavor to have somebody else's experiences, write someone else's books, or take on someone else's spiritual journey. This often results in further deception as we "succeed" in becoming someone we are not. As a people, we are in a hurry to magnify ourselves by imitating what is popular—and are too lazy to think of anything better or unique. In other words, without thinking we blindly accept the conventional cultural narrative assigned us by the social and choice architects tasked to create us into persons making their system flourish.

Speed and hurry ruin us. We want quick success and we are in such a hurry to get it that we cannot slow down enough to become our true selves. We would rather settle for pseudo and shallow success via imitation than live a smaller life by cultural standards while remaining true to the self, because remaining true to the self is harder work. And when we are lost or even at home among the chaos, busyness, and speed we become so deceived that we argue and defend that our very busyness and speed is the basis for our success. The irony in this is that we end up succeeding at becoming a stranger to who we were meant to be.

To insist on being someone other than our true self is a matter of great pride, for it is to insist that we know better than God, the God who made us to be our unique selves. This sort of pride lays at the foundation of the severe identity crisis many of us wake up with around midlife. We realize we are lost, which should not surprise us, for up to this point we have committed our energies to travel another person's journeys.

The irony is that the more the false self grows in strength, at the same time the true self, the self that God breathes into existence, dwindles to the point there is nothing left of us to live on into God's eternal kingdom.

Existing and thriving as our false self in the here and now is at the same time a sentencing to nonexistence. However, the discovery of our true self is found as God begins to name and reveal the false self for what it is. When God begins to reveal this we are left with the option of retreating back into the false self, which is a living death, or stepping out into the true self that is contained within the Divine.

In order for one to become their true self, we must begin to step through thresholds that seem very unfamiliar, maybe even taboo or heretical. We must willfully cease to be what we always thought we wanted to be, and in order to find and thus live out of our true self we must, in the words of Jesus, "deny our self."[2] As the false self begins to die, then Christ, with whom the true self is hidden within, begins to live.[3] Christ must take control of directing each individual's personhood, as opposed to self-centered ambitions. Now, let's take a peek into the world of geography.

Mechanical Weathering

There is a process in the world of geography called "mechanical weathering." Mechanical weathering is a slow process that causes big and seemingly unbreakable rocks to actually break. The process gradually takes place due to the ebb and flow of warm days and cool nights, which leads to a rhythm of contraction and expansion. This process creates small cracks that begin on the surface of the rock and weave themselves toward the center. As the cracks form, space is created for another process to take place, called the freeze-thaw. Essentially, when it rains, water lands on the surface of the rock and seeps into and through the cracks. With no place to go, the water simply rests, and then during the cold nights the water freezes and expands, leading to the eventual breaking apart of the large rock.

This, from my experience, is how the transformative truth of the Divine works. Often times our experiences and circumstances, especially when we subject ourselves to contexts and situations we are not accustomed to, act as mechanical weathering in our life. Metaphorical cracks are formed that lead to the center of our false self. On a side note, when we do not subject ourselves to situations and contexts that we are not comfortable with, we are protecting ourselves from the work of the Spirit in our lives, and ironically, in the name of God we prevent ourselves from being

2. Matthew 16:24–26.

3. Galatians 2:19–21.

transformed into the true self God has preordained. Truth acts as the water that hits the surface of the rock and finds its way into the cracks. For a long time it doesn't seem like truth is doing anything. As we travel through different seasons in life, the truth hiding within the cracks begins to freeze and expand, and eventually the large rock or our seemingly unshakable false self begins to break apart. This process is exactly what was happening in my soul that would lead to a meltdown upon the realization that my understanding of reality was not as solid as I thought it was.

It Began in Ecclesiastes

I was teaching through the book of Ecclesiastes when a particular passage stunned me. I had read this passage several times. But for some reason, this time it hit me more like an epiphany. I'm not sure if it was because my self-created path was in such opposition to this sort of text or because after years of work my false self had reached a point of unsustainable fragility, due to the Spirit making headway into the center of my false self—probably both.

In Ecclesiastes 7:2 we read that it "is better to go to the house of mourning than to the house of feasting; for this is the end of everyone, and the living will lay it to heart." This is not the way we live in our society. Our lives are motivated by illusion of limitlessness and unreal capacity. But we are not limitless, nor are our visions, nor is life. Life is limited. We are mortal. And the only thing that will outlive us on this earth is the story we tell with our lives, the story that will be passed on by our children and their children, and their children's children. And according to Ecclesiastes, I was living my life from the wrong vantage point. I wonder if this one verse holds within it the reason so many of us come to a midlife crisis. Maybe this is what Thomas Merton meant when he said, "People may spend their whole lives climbing the ladder of success only to find once they reach the top, that the ladder is leaning against the wrong wall."

My Tipping Point

By definition, a tipping point is the critical point in a situation, process, or system beyond which a significant and often unstoppable effect or change takes place.[4] Based on that definition, I was at my tipping point. I knew it.

4. *Merriam-Webster*, s.v. "Tipping Point," https://www.merriam-webster.com/diction ary/tipping%20point.

I knew I was lost. I knew I was not following truth. I knew I had come to a fork in the road. The one thing I hadn't done yet was verbalize this knowledge outside of my home.

Sometimes verbalizing something, speaking it out, makes it more real. Speaking sometimes makes tangible what we already know to be true. I was in that same van, the van where the questioning of reality began, but this time I was not staring into oblivion. I was in the middle of a very fun day. Sarah was in Ecuador doing some research and supply chain transparency work for a company out of Austin. So, myself and a couple other friends took our kids to a nearby pumpkin patch. It was a great day, and on the way home Kari, a great friend of ours, was riding back with me. As typical with her, our conversations turn deep quickly, and some way we had arrived on a conversation about identity. She asked me a very simple, ordinary, seemingly non-consequential question. "If you don't think you are being true to yourself, then who is your true self?" That's it, that's all she asked me. But something about responding out loud with "I don't know" sent me over the edge. To mix metaphors, this was my tipping point, this was the final drop of rain that froze within the cracks of my false self that caused me to realize I had a heavy choice to make.

Would I ignore what was going on internally and turn back to the life I had made, drown out and thus suffocate the voices calling me to a different road, or would I step through the threshold to the place of liminality? Would I be "responsible" or step off the beaten path down the road that would first call me to the journey of undoing my false self, while at the same time slowly resurrecting the person I was meant to be? We chose the threshold that lead us into the liminal realm. Our first step on this journey was questioning everything, even the very nature and existence of God. So, I leave you with two questions. Back at the beginning of the chapter, I described how I was faced with the question, "What if it doesn't get any better than this?" My awakening and crisis came into being as I learned to define my "it" and my "better." What is your "it"? What is your "better"?

Chapter 3: Liminality: The Undefinable Now

I had heard of you by the hearing of my ear, but now my eye sees you; therefore I refuse myself and am comforted in dust and ash.

—Job

Theodicy may be the most prideful and disillusioned assertion we make as human beings. To defend God, which is to assume the Divine even needs our defense, is beyond our ability and surpasses our pay grade as humans. In his work *A Grief Observed*, Lewis asserts, "Not that I am (I think) in much danger of ceasing to believe in God. The real danger is of coming to believe such dreadful things about Him. The conclusion I dread is not 'So there's no God after all,' but 'So this is what God's really like.'"[1]

If we engage God and life with any ounce of intellectual integrity, we have to, like Lewis, come to some sort of conclusion that leaves us wanting. Maybe it isn't that God is bad, maybe it we are still in need of painful shaping. Or maybe the divine is not what we thought it was. We long for a one-dimensional-answers to a multidimensional life. We simply think if we can figure out the "why" behind the tension, pain, and confusion the remedy or solution will then be abreast. Yet we know this is not true. The reason why she cheated on him doesn't dull the pain, it doesn't erase the insecurity, or decrease the grief; it's just information that clutters it all. It doesn't matter that she says, "It wasn't good. It's not you, it's me. I still love you, he meant nothing to me." All has changed. No amount of explanation results in a calming and satisfactory understanding. Everything prior is now tainted and carries with it a shadow.

It seems to me religious arrogance when we assert some sort of divine sovereignty in times of grief and sorrow that is onset by untimely death, the

---

1. Lewis, *Grief Observed*, 6.

loss of a child or loved one, or the shattering of innocence. The cute phrase "God has a plan for your life" delivers little comfort when you've worked hard for something for over twenty years only to find yourself less sure and emptier than you were when you started. However, on the flip side, this is just what we do as humans. We look for remedies, we look to solve problems, we need that which seems contradictory to be put to right. But it can't be, at least not in this realm. Sometimes, and I think most the time, the best thing we can do in these times of irreconcilable tensions, confusions, or devastation is to sit with it. We don't need to explain it away. We don't need to numb it. We don't need it to make sense, we need to let it be what it is. We need to sit with it, until it is over, until something in us or our entire being is transformed during this undefinable now.

In the ancient Hebrew texts, when a community or a person found themselves in a place of loss or devastation or sin or confusion, they didn't try to solve it, rather they entered into ritualistic mourning. They would tear their clothes and put dust and ash on their heads and they would sit with it—they would let it be what it was until it had its effect. That's not to say that there isn't a time to act—there absolutely is—but we all know, at least those of us who have attempted to do the hardest thing there is to do in these times, which I will call the undefinable now, and sit with it, when we allow ourselves to submit to these times, we end up changed, and we come out transformed. We are scarred and yet matured. We are darker and yet contain a deeper and thicker joy. This is the theme of my favorite book in the Bible, Job.

We love to water down the story of Job, or maybe not so much water it down as much as give God his "get out of jail free" card, the card that allows us to keep him boxed in our dualistic categories of "good" and "evil"—Satan and sin cause evil and pain, God and obedience cause favor and abundance. While this is the wisdom of the young author of Proverbs, it is not the aged wisdom we read in books like Ecclesiastes and Job. Job goes through much pain, loss, and confusion and thus is resolute on avoiding an easy solution. In fact, the causality of Job's pain, according to the author, is clearly God.[2] Through the majority of the book, we have dialogues between Job and his friends attempting to make sense of the chaos and pain. The tactics employed through the book are the old faithful ones that we employ today, such as judging, logic, tradition, and casting blame, and at the end all of their ability to defend God and make sense of this undefinable now in the

2. Job 1:8–12; 2:1–10; 42:11.

life of Job fails them. God never satisfies them with a logical answer, nor does he explain away their assertions about the Divine. If anything, God, toward the end of the book, seems satisfied with basically telling them they are too ignorant to understand, and reminds them of who he is and who they are not. If Job tells us anything, it's that we cannot explain away the undefinable now. We can't fix it. But something is happening in it. We are either dying or we are being transformed and maybe both. At the end of the story, after Job made it to the other side of his undefinable now, he says, "I had heard of you by the hearing of my ear, but now my eye sees you; therefore I refuse myself and am comforted in dust and ash."[3] In the most devastating time of his life, he held on, he sat with it, and came out on the other side transformed. This is the liminal journey.

The liminal journey is found through all the great myths and many of the stories that we love today. It seems that it was never to be an optional path, but one destined for us all. In C. S. Lewis' *Till We Have Faces*, Orual, the ugly and oldest sister who is destined to be Queen, plays the role of narrator. She begins the book as sort of a rage against the gods because she is not like Psyche her younger sister. By the second half of the book, she is coming through her liminal journey that is talked about as dreams of tasks that begin to be actualized in the daytime. These dreams are the part of her journey that are the undoing of her false-self, and it is within these dreams that she is confronted not just with who god is, but with her true self. Orual believes the issue is with the god; she is looking for a theodicy-type answer. This is not where the transformation happens. The god brings her to a place of higher knowing through transformation in the place of liminality. After coming to the realization as to what has actually been going on and making her final complaint, to the god causing all of this pain for her good, she says, "I know now, Lord, why you utter no answer. You are yourself the answer. Before your face questions die away. What other answer would suffice?"[4]

Orual's life can best be summed up with a quote from Joseph Campbell: "Where we had thought to find abomination, we shall find a god; where we had thought to slay another, we shall slay ourselves; where we had thought to travel outward, we shall come to the center of our own existence; where we had thought to be alone, we shall be with the world."[5] This is our journey.

3. Job 42:2–6.

4. Lewis, *Till We Have Faces*, 307.

5. Campbell, *Hero with a Thousand Faces*, 15.

This was Job's journey. This was Orual's journey. The liminal journey, though often expressed outward, is truly inward. Doesn't Jesus say the kingdom of God is within you? It is this kingdom within us that is slowly fighting and defeating the ego-kingdom we have been attempting to architect. The liminal journey is about slaying or the undoing of the false self, and it is through this journey and through this journey alone that we are reunited or resurrected back into the world, to finally be who we were meant to be.

Liminality in its most basic idea is an in-between state where one's identity is being recreated.[6] You are not where you were, and you are not where you are going; you are in the borderlands, the in-between, or the undefinable now. And as a person, you probably have or probably will become more ambiguous.

Often times through life we lose who we are or come to the end of one season in our life, as I noted in my journal entry at the beginning of the book. This can happen for various reasons, but at the end of the day, it is often a result of the everyday negotiation between the identity society and/or culture project on us and who we are at our core. We enter the world of compromise. Then at some point in the lived-out negotiation, we make a deal or a trade that is too steep, often both unintentionally and unbeknownst to ourselves. Subconsciously, we know if we want to make it and succeed, whatever that means in your context, in our current realm, we have to reconstruct a version of ourselves that bows to the system making the demands upon us. A social identity is created at the expense of the true self, all because we have bought into an illusion that promises something it will never deliver. This is often a slow process and guided by the ego-self banking on the idea that at some point in the future you will have arrived at a place in time or status that will allow you to simply step out of the illusion back into the you you long to be. It assumes—here's the ego part—that while this happens to so many others, it won't happen to me. And then one day you wake up realizing you are not who you want to be or thought you would be back when you made the trade. Our culture has a term for this point in life: "midlife crisis." Midlife crisis is typically defined as a crisis we come to when we haven't achieved or ascended to our version of the American dream like everyone else around us.

On one hand, that's exactly what it is: a crisis, a crisis of the self. On the other hand, our culture—fast paced, production based, consumeristic in nature—is not going to allow us to think that it is okay to engage the crisis.

6. Beech, "Liminality and the Practices of Identity Reconstruction," 64.

Like pain when touching a hot stove, the crisis is actually communicating something of importance to us. Our society, driving corporatism and hypercapitalistic systems, need us to regain or hold on to the ego-self, the false self, the self that was birthed out of our affair with the illusion—whether that illusion is the promises made to you from the corporate world, the church world, the world of academia, or even promised joys if you submit to projected gender roles—that the system projects in order to keep us working in a way that actually sustains the system at our own expense. We will be told we need to medicate ourselves to get beyond it. We will be told we need to go to an in-network therapist that will help us come to grips with who we were and convince us that it is okay to remain that way. Or, and I think this is the most common experience, we will guilt and shame ourselves back to the shore we are being called to leave. We will look around and see the culturally defined success of all the others in our field, and convince ourselves that it is just us, and if we push harder, power through, or pray more, then we will get through this, and all will be fine. Nobody tells us that, more often than not, midlife, or whatever we want to call it, is actually an invitation into the liminal journey.

However, the invitation to the liminal journey is typically triggered by some sort of event that causes us to step outside of our self delivers a haunting feeling that everything, even if it looks like it, is not okay, nor should it be. This event can be a death of a loved one, the loss of a job, an affair, or even being opened up to new realities we were previously ignorant of. The safe thing, the more commonly practiced action, is to deafen our ears to the dark call of the liminal journey by burying ourselves in more work, consuming more, and starting new projects. The liminal space is scary, because it is the place that begins to strip and deconstruct us in a journey of descent.[7]

Once entered, you can never go back to the way things were. If you throw in the towel, and attempt to go back, you will go back to a shadow of the person you were. Existentially speaking, to go back is to be stuck in the journey you never completed and the other half will be trying to forget it while living a normal life. So, my suggestion is, take the liminal journey, walk through the dark threshold and don't look back; or don't at all, and turn a deaf ear to the call and submerse yourself in the world as you know it. Caution: if we do ignore the call, we will indeed fall back, and begin to idolize and justify the cultural norms that actually insulate

7. Rohr, *Everything Belongs*, 46.

us and thus protect us from the true self awaiting to emerge on the other side of the journey.[8]

As mentioned above, the liminal space is entered as we move into the realm between two worlds—where you were and where you are going. This in-between place is where passage rites happen—in other words, it is a place where we are being initiated for a new world. According to the late cultural anthropologist Victor Turner, the liminal journey is marked by three phases: separation, marginalization, and aggregation.[9]

Separation

The first phase, separation, doesn't necessarily or even initially happen geographically, it often begins internally through some sort of realization, an uneasy feeling, or a chronic tension of some sort. This is often where the journey begins or ends for many. For many of us, we will ignore or suppress the realization or the tension by pushing through business as usual or convincing ourselves we are wrong. If we ignore it, all is not lost. God is so intent on our transformation that the universe will continually bring us around to points of disruption or forks in the road where we are forced to ignore or embrace the tension.

This is what Sarah and I came to when we had the discussion of "falling off the grid." Something wasn't right, but we didn't know what. And that is often the roadblock for many: we could not come up with objective evidence to justify or convince ourselves that we had permission to do just that, enter the liminal by "falling off the grid." Moving into the liminal space is voluntary displacement. In our culture we have to chose to go against the societal norm and willfully, often against conventional wisdom, walk through the threshold. There will always be a million excuses and reasons not to go, but at the end of the day, the choice is ours. We have to, so to speak, pay attention to the call and induce the crisis that seems to be calling us. The liminal journey always begins with the experience of displacement, with the hope of transformation.[10] While I suggest that the internal separation be actualized through social, geographic, and vocational separation, I'm not sure I believe it is necessary, but it certainly does allow for the gravity of the separation to be felt deeper and makes it much more difficult to

8. Rohr, *Everything Belongs*, 155.

9. Turner, *Ritual Process*, 94.

10. Rohr, *Everything Belongs*, 49–50.

turn back. When tangible separation happens, a line is drawn in the sand. There is the time before the separation and the time after. There is a distinguishable then and the undefinable now.

Marginalization

The phase of separation is followed by the space where we are being separated unto a place, and that is the place of marginalization. Marginalization is the place where one begins to detach from the fixed points in our lives—the cultural ethos, systems, structures and networks that feed and influence the rhythms we were committed to—and step into a realm that has few, if any, of the attributes and rhythms that the ego-self so readily feeds and depends on.[11]

It is here in the place of marginalization that panic and stress usually begins to take hold of our heart. Every decision one makes to facilitate this process will seem foolish. The loudest voices in your life will be those telling you to run back to the other shore, and they will drown out the wisdom that told you to trust the process and embrace liminality. In the place of marginalization we are being "ground down or reduced" to our most basic or primal self, the place where weakness is our greatest strength. The hope is that this is happening so that we can be "born again" or reshaped with both an internal peace and maturity as well as the wisdom, which often replaces what some would call "strength," to live deep and well on the new shore that we will eventually be spit up on.[12] This is the ethos of this part of the liminal journey—stripping away. We, those who find ourselves committed to the undefinable now, must take on the posture of humility and submission in order to allow God's transformative hand to have its intended effect.[13] It is here that I experienced the apophatic nature of God, which I will delve into more in the next chapter.

If, like myself, you are a get-it-done personality and you thrive on taking control and making things happen, you are in for a battle, a battle in which the only way to be truly successful is to lose. You have to arrive at the place where you are willing to allow marginalization to happen to you rather than exerting yourself on it. Rohr equates the marginalization portion of liminality to the metaphor of Jonah in belly of the whale. Our

11. Turner, *Ritual Process*, 94.

12. Turner, *Ritual Process*, 95.

13. Turner, *Ritual Process*, 102–3.

society provides us with several ways to escape and justifications to avoid the belly of the whale, through shallow calls to success, notoriety, fame, along with fear based propaganda reminding us of all we will give up and miss out on if we leave this shore for another, especially if the threshold we are walking into is an undefinable now. Sure, it is easier to wait and leave one shore if we know and see the next, but that's now what liminality is about. It is about trusting the process and letting go of the outcome. It's committing to a journey without knowing the destination. However, when we choose to escape this path, we are not so much escaping actual danger, rather we are escaping the place where deep and lasting transformation happens. In the belly of the whale, Jonah's previous accomplishments, accolades, networks, education, or whatever else we take pride in didn't matter—the whale didn't care. The whale didn't care who Jonah knew before this or how many books he had written or had written about him. It didn't matter in the belly of the whale that Jonah was known as a great prophet; Jonah's status had been reduced to plankton. Jonah had been stripped down and left with no bargaining tools except himself.

Once Jonah was stripped of everything, the belly of the great fish became the locality of transformation and refinement. According to Rohr, this is the great teaching space, the space in which, if we trust our time in it without needing to fix, control, or even understand it, in due time God will "spit us out" on new shores, and we will re-emerge as our true self.[14]

Aggregation

The third and final phase is aggregation. This is where and when transcendence begins to happen. The actual word "aggregation" means the condition of being collected through the many parts that create a whole.[15] In other words, the undefinable now begins to gain some shape and thus the ability to define all that lays ahead, and often what came before. This experience transcends the now as you move into this second part of your life.[16] In this phase all that has survived the stripping, which is more or less what is left or what has been revealed about the true self and what has been learned

14. Rohr and Martos, *From Wild Man to Wise Man*, 84.

15. *Merriam-Webster*, s.v. "aggregation," http://www.merriam-webster.com/dictionary/aggregation.

16. Turner, *Ritual Process*, 95.

and gained through the liminal journey, begins to merge together to form and reveal the whole of who we are.

There's a story in Mark's gospel about Jesus healing a blind man that really encompasses the stages of liminality. What we know, based on the high esteem to which Jesus was held by the early church, is that the recording of the story could have simply been summed up as Jesus touching the man to heal him, while leaving out the detail of village separation, mud, and spit. But the author doesn't do this. If Jesus wanted us to skip the separation and the marginalization, he could simply make it happen, and while we often beg him to remove us from these places, he doesn't. So, Jesus separates the man from the village, from the place which has surely projected a social identity upon him, an identity that he had internally adopted and came to accept.[17] Jesus spits in dirt and makes a paste, and wipes it on the man's eyes—restoration via humiliation. I wasn't there, I don't know if the man actually felt humiliated, but I'm pretty sure, with a second layer of blindness, mud made by spit, and separation from the identity he had come to accept about himself, marginalization would be a pretty fair way to define this moment in this man's existence. Jesus begins to move the man out of this space, but a new view on reality is not immediate; he cannot see clearly yet.[18] Like the blind man, we can see there is another shore, we can see that we may be approaching a new world, we can even see that our reflection is different than it was prior to this liminal space, but it is not yet clear what it is we see. This is what it is like to move into the phase of aggregation. We can't yet see or know clearly, but we can see something.

The nakedness, humiliations, utter weakness, and loneliness that are submitted to in the place of marginalization are now being revealed, not as tortures from heaven's jester, but as tools used to bring our previous status and ego-self into destruction so that they can no longer contaminate the true self, the self that is being reformed and developed for our new world. We have now come to the understanding that all we pridefully clung to as our identity were simply particles of dust and clay that had been socially impressed on us in order to live out that portion of our life.[19] They, the dust and clay, were not in and of themselves evil, they did not become destructive until we decided they would override and dictate the true self. The consciousness and wisdom that is gained within this place of liminality is an ontological aggregation at

17. John 9:1-2; Leviticus 21:18; Mark 10:46–52.
18. Mark 8:24.
19. Turner, *Ritual Process*, 103.

its core, in that it has refashioned the very being of those of us who have willingly embarked into the undefined now.[20]

As mentioned above, our society not only makes it possible to avoid liminality, but rewards those who do. If you find yourself in liminal space and have allowed the dominant social narrative to convince you that you have failed, fallen apart, or simply missed it; don't. If you are contemplating the road offered to you by culture, the road laced with a modern definition of success, false notions of accomplishments, and illusions of safety; don't. By the time you realize you should have entered the road less traveled, it may be too late. While this road can feel very lonely, to travel into the undefined now, like many of the great and difficult hiking trails, you will be in good company. I do not deny the extreme difficulty of this journey—it was extremely difficult, as reflected in my journal entry above, but writing from the other side of it, I can tell you it was worth it.

We begin the liminal journey in search of deep answers or to find our true self. We spend much time shaking our frail fists and making accusations against the gods, but like Job, Orual, and myself, we pass through this dark night of the soul, embrace the apophatic experience, and echo Job as we move from a person who had heard of God to a person who can say to the Divine, "Now my eye sees you."

As we move closer to the center of the book, have you stopped to ask yourself, "What do I need to let go of, or distance myself from?" If you haven't, do so before you move on to the next chapter.

20. Turner, *Ritual Process*, 103.

Chapter 4: **Apophatic: The Darkside of God**

Not that I am (I think) in much danger of ceasing to believe in God.
The real danger is of coming to believe such dreadful things about
Him. The conclusion I dread is not "So there's no God after all," but "So
this is what God's really like. Deceive yourself no longer."

—C. S. Lewis, *A Grief Observed*

My God, my God, why have you forsaken me?

—Jesus[1]

When life seems to be spinning out of control, and one's emotional
bubble seems to be rupturing at the seams, the tried and true response, the one that has "worked" for decades, is to "run to God in prayer"
or simply to abandon all and rest in the shadows of his wings.[2] But what
happens when all you feel is the shadow?

There's a term in physics known as "negative matter." It's the type of
language used in discussion about wormholes and black holes.[3] I don't
want to get into the depth of this idea, nor am I qualified to, but in essence
the idea of negative matter is when the nothingness, or the darkness or
the emptiness, is substance. It is weighty and has a gravitational pull to
it. It is not simply the absence of something, it is the weighty presence of
nothingness.

For those of you who are of the Christian faith, like myself, we have all
experienced the absence of God. For many this is seasonal—in other words,

1. Matthew 27:46.
2. Psalm 36:7.
3. Belletete and Paranjape, "On Negative Mass."

we can go months, even years, and never feel the presence of God. That idea was not new to me, and unfortunately all too common. But that's not what I was experiencing. The negation or absence of God had weight to it, it had gravitational pull; there was a substance to it that I still have a hard time explaining. As far as I knew, my faith history had nothing to say about this. I was honestly wondering if I was losing my faith. Was God rejecting me? To identify or best describe this experience, I had to turn to physics to find the necessary terminology I needed to define this darkness—negative matter. Yet, even this seemed limiting, because presence is not matter, it is more like energy, and in the past when God seemed absent, it was just the absence of energy; but now, this, this was negative energy.

I was attempting to explain this to a professor friend of mine and he just smiled. I didn't think it was too funny. He simply said, "Oh, yes, Christianity has a rich heritage of this. We call it apophatic theology, and it seems, my friend, that God is bringing you through an apophatic experience. Don't fight it." He then went on to point me to the writings of Basil the Great, Gregory of Nyssa, Gregory of Nazianzua, John Chrysostom, John of Damascus, and many others. In short, apophatic theology is a theological position that is as old as the Cappadocian Fathers and simply reveals the inability of our doctrines, theologies, and languages to speak adequately about the dark side of God.[4] When we take this to the experiential level, we are simply saying that the practices, theories, and even places where we were once comforted the most by God's presence no longer encapsulate the presence of the Divine—in other words, they no longer work. The practices that once brought comfort, were now haunting. Rather than being comforted by the presence or energy of God I now feel the weight of his negative energy. My religious symbols and practices no longer worked. I could no longer sense God inside of me rather, I was experiencing the "negative matter" of God. I was being pulled into what seemed like a weighty nothingness.

My whole life, as far back as I can remember, I took great pride in the fact that I seemed to be a natural ascetic. But what happens when the religious fervor, symbols, and localities as to where one has historically met God begin to fail? What happens when all you experience is the darkness of his shadow? I was coming to the realization that the places, ideas, thoughts, and practices that I hung my assurance on were not necessarily the places God was, rather they were semiotic relationships put together, probably by my

---

4. McGrath, "Apophatic Theology and Masculinities," 503.

subconscious, to form systems in which I felt safe with the god I had learned to manage, and probably create.

We know there is no human theology, quantifiable doctrine, or language that adequately defines the Divine. In the same measure there is no adequate discipline or set of ascetic practices that allows one to fully know God in the complete depth of ultimate reality. The apophatic mode rejects our prefabricated models, and when God begins to move one into this realm, the divine energy begins to turn the very ways and methods that were once our safeguard on their head. The Divine not only deconstructs our previously relied upon methods, he reveals them to be obstacles that are standing in the way of our movement toward him.[5] This is not to say that one will not reclaim some of the practices that were at one time comforting, it is simply to say that God may, for a season, remove them. This was my experience.

For me, the places that I met the presence of God most frequently were in the Christian Scriptures, prayer, and silence. I looked forward to these, I would go to bed longing for them. They fueled me with energy and insight. Now God seemed like the great thief, as one by one the negative energy consumed these elements and took them from my comfort. They were no longer places of peace but dark halls of anguish. Sitting in silence was no longer acceptable for me, the silence had become daunting and scary, my mind was full of a darkness that I could not escape. Scripture was rendered mute—no matter how much I read a line, I could not, for the life of me, tell you what I had read, much less what it meant. There was no life or comfort within the words of the text, only a constant reminder that I was very lost. Prayer was mental and emotional noise. To verbally attempt to communicate with this divine energy seemed like a feat of strength that I could not muster from within. It seemed that the only life I could muster was in avoiding time alone with God.

People would ask me, "Do you not feel God at all?" I would say, "No, but oddly, I feel like I can see the Divine. I feel as if the Divine is hiding in the unlikely faces and landscapes around me. When I am there, among them I am, it feels, with God. Though, like an introverted stranger in a room, God does not make eye contact with me; just simply lets me see evidence of the mystery." Basically, what God was doing, and is always doing at some level, if we are open to it, was exposing the inability of my leaned-upon disciplines and system to adequately contain and know the Divine, in order to actually

5. Beachy-Quick, "Apophatic."

move me closer within him.[6] This was, looking back, the shadow side of divine grace. In God's grace, I was going through a kenotic process, in that I was being emptied of the thoughts, patterns, categories, and images, as well as the locality of where I knew God, in order to know God more deeply.[7]

Lost and alone is the best way I know to communicate how I felt. I couldn't stand to be alone, and as an introvert that is not a good place to be. But it seemed the only way I could sense a hint of the Divine was real in the faces of people. As a pastor this is not an experience I had made plans for. Maybe I should have, but this is not the stuff that our networks or denominations prepare us for. We need to build churches, we need growth tactics, and we need to create models for sustainability. The church planters graveyard is full of men and women who started with the excitement of the kingdom and got lost in apophatic abyss. They did not have people around them to help them through, and when they talked about it, those they were supposed to rely on didn't know what to do.

Joseph Campbell talks about attending psychological conferences dealing with the problem or the fine line between mystical experience and psychological crack-ups, and he says, "the difference is that the one who cracks up is drowning in the water in which mystics swim. You have to be prepared for this experience."[8] I was drowning in waters that I was meant to swim in. The church was never supposed to be about building a religious business. When our pastors, who have been trained for religious corporations, are confronted with the transcendent, mystical, and powerful reality of God, they are not prepared for anything that calls them out of the controllable realms, and they end up drowning.

I was fortunate enough to have the right people around me—my family, spiritual directors, friends, professors, and counselors who seemed to have been through this stuff, as well as access to great literature. The greatest single piece of literature that helped me the most, if for no other reason than it gave insight and verbiage to what I was going through, was Christian Wiman's *My Bright Abyss*.

While Wiman writes about his interior experience as both an intellectual and one fighting cancer, he seems to deeply grapple with many of the faith issues I was struggling with and had struggled with much of my adult life. Wiman was not my sole literary guide, giving literary expression to my

6. McGrath, "Apophatic Theology and Masculinities," 504.

7. Beachy-Quick, "Apophatic."

8. Campbell and Moyers, *Power of Myth*, 16.

interior aching. I found meaning in the writings of Joseph Campbell, who gave locality for this struggle within my Christian walk, and Richard Rohr's masculine spirituality that acted as a bridge between Wiman's expression and Campbell's narrative arch.

As we were preparing to leave Austin, I was talking with another local church planter, Jonathan Dodson, who planted his church the same year we did, about what I was struggling with and the journey I felt I was embarking on. He responded in two ways. The first was, in his typical and believable sincere way, to let me know he would be praying for me. For many, when we get the response "I'll be praying for you," we know it's not much more than a kind gesture, but that's not the way it was with Jonathan. When Jonathan said, "Man, I'll be praying for you," you believed it, you knew he would be. There is something refreshing about knowing you have these sorts of people in your life, whom you can confess to, and they won't try to fix it—they simply let you know, "I'm going to share that burden, and I'm going to pray for you." The other thing he did was shoot me an email that contained a scanned version of a spiritual roadmap. The map was an outline of Richard Rohr's idea of the spiritual journey, which follows Campbell's outline of the hero's journey.[9] This outline indicated that somewhere between the ages of thirty-five and fifty we reach a place that Rohr calls "Crisis of Limitation," and Campbell refers to this as a "threshold," the door into the "special world," or darkness. We come to a point, if we are honoring of the voice that is calling us into the void, in which we begin to face our true self, which is often at war with our false self.[10] The difference between this face off is not so much found in its unique occurrence, rather it is found in the revelation of weakness. I was beginning to face the dark side of who I wasn't. Losing was more prominent than winning. Failing seemed to become habit. Loneliness was prevalent even among those I loved. I was, as we all should, crossing a threshold in which my lived in reality was a constant reminder of my overshadowing limitations. The realization we face or the truth we come to is that there can be great inner growth and strength in pure agony or destruction—the destruction is of the false self.[11]

This place is so painful that we have created paths within our culture and society to help us avoid it. In fact, those who can't avoid it are perceived

9. Rohr and Martos, *From Wild Man to Wise Man*, 164–66.

10. Romans 7:15–20.

11. Wiman, *My Bright Abyss*, 19.

as failures and weak. Yet, to avoid it is not to follow God, but rather a projected and defied version of our false self that keeps us believing that the way up is, indeed, the way forward, when in truth the way forward may be a way into being more eternally lost.

God is in the business of undoing. The first part of life, the concept of God is often a better and even deified version of the false self. God is like a blank screen and we project our self onto him—it's why he rarely disagrees with us, it's why the God of the Old Testament always seemed to not only approve of, but command, the violence of Israel. The same is true for us: we project ourselves onto the blank screen we call "God" and then we worship it and this god continually affirms what we believe and the ambitions of our lives. This becomes our truth. And while God meets us here and allows himself to be disguised as this god, the real God is behind the scenes of our lives, calling us to a sort of unbelief so that a real faith in the ultimate Divine can take shape. Consequently, our faith begins to take new forms.[12]

When we let go, we return to the place of innocence. We are now like babes again. All that we have put our faith in, in the name of God—platform, fame, education, networks, methods, etc.—has failed to support our interior life. We are faced with two options: first, in pride and fear, we dig our heels in, and we fight and thus live the rest of our lives as old fools, or the person who has been equipped, often by the church, to actually avoid the apophatic journey in order to worship their projected god. Or, second, we admit, we confess our doubt and innocence and thus our total weakness, which seems to be the place God is constantly directing the saints.[13] Doubt, innocence, and weakness bring us back to hearing God—not our filtered version of the Divine, but God, where we are "rendered mute with awe, fear, wonder."[14]

I said earlier in this chapter that God seemed intent on escaping my relied upon practices and hid in the faces and landscapes around me. According to Wiman, this is exactly what God does, and this is what God is doing; by subtracting the divine energy from one part of your life, you are being moved toward the world and other people, along with your true self.[15]

Typically, when we experience moments like this, we are motivated by some sort of distinct finish, a complete end to it. Wiman says, ". . . the turn toward God has not lessened my anxieties, and I find myself continually falling

---

12. Wiman, *My Bright Abyss*, 61.

13. Job 42:1–6; 2 Corinthians 12:8–10.

14. Wiman, *My Bright Abyss*, 71.

15. Wiman, *My Bright Abyss*, 76.

back into wounds, wishes, terrors I thought I had risen beyond."[16] This is not a bad thing. To struggle is proof that we are moving forward. However, to add to Wiman's thought, as maybe an encouragement to move forward for those who feel lost in or are entering the apophatic journey: Do not avoid it. Do not ignore the demons. Own your weakness, and rest in it, know God in it. You will feel like the odd person out. You will feel like a failure. If God is using, anxiety, failure, stress, depression, illness, loss, or even absence to invite you into the dark journey where you will be confronted with the negative matter of the soul, then I urge you to go, and don't give up.

The true contemplatives, such as Thomas Merton, have been telling us this for generations. The living God, the god who is God, and cannot be reduced to a philosophical or theoretical abstract idea, a pronoun, nor a safe Christian frame, lies infinitely beyond the reach of anything we can see or understand. No matter what sound theological idea we predicate of him, we have to add that our concept is only a shadow of the true God, and our conception of the divine is at best extremely limited in every way.[17]

Merton tells us, "He who is infinite light is so tremendous in His evidence" that as the Divine allows us to get a peek into ultimate reality, "our minds only see Him as darkness."[18] Merton continues this line of thought by saying, "If nothing that can be seen can either be God or represent Him to us as He is, then to find God we must pass beyond everything that can be seen and enter into darkness. Since nothing that can be heard is God, to find Him we must enter into silence. Since God cannot be imagined, anything our imagination tells us about Him is ultimately misleading and therefore we cannot know Him as He really is unless we pass beyond everything that can be imagined and enter into an obscurity without images and without the likeness of any created thing."[19] Merton is describing this apophatic experience that we must pass through as we embrace liminality.

Like a phoenix who has been brought to ash, we are brought to ash by the darkside of God, and we are then invited into discovery and a newness. We are now left with a vision of the true self, as we begin to journey toward ontological wholeness.

16. Wiman, *My Bright Abyss*, 9.

17. 1 Corinthians 3:9–12.

18. Merton, *New Seeds of Contemplation*, 131.

19. Merton, *New Seeds of Contemplation*, 131.

Chapter 5: **Ontological Wholeness**

All resistance is a rupture with what is. And every rupture begins, for those engaged in it, through a rupture with oneself.

—ALAIN BADIOU, *METAPOLITICS*

I end each year praying for a "word" from God. Not so much like a special epiphany, as much as an actual word: grace, mercy, joy, repentance, and so on. Once I believe God has given me that word, I look for a few texts that pertain to that word, and then figure out a summarized version of that text, so that I have a short thought or sentence to return to while meditating or praying throughout the day. The purpose behind this request for a word is all about intentionally participating in the way God is shaping me. For instance, if I feel like the "word of the year" is "grace," I assume, typically, that God is going to teach me to have more grace on others. This typically comes as God invites me to become more real about my own brokenness by also revealing the grace I have been granted and need to live in my day to day life. In light of that, I may find a text like 2 Corinthians 12:9, which states, "your grace is enough." This text will become like a mantra for me: I will use it as a mini repeated prayer during the day. I will say it over and over when my actions are proving that I don't actually believe the grace of God is enough, I will say it when I believe a person needs to pay for what they have done before our relationship can be restored. And for twenty-three minutes every morning I will meditate on it. In short, I will saturate my life for a whole year reflecting on the many aspects of grace.

I've been doing this for close to a decade now and it seems to really help out in the way of spiritual development, particularly as it creates a framework and lens to view and interact with the world around me. Since I've been doing this, I have spent whole years focusing on things like grace, mercy, patience, faith, and holiness. However, about four years ago I received a word that lasted about two years. A word that took me off guard. A word that I had, in the past, considered an attribute to be avoided. A word that should never be on anyone's value list; or so I assumed. That word is "weakness."

In chapter 1, entitled "Disillusioned," I refer to a conversation between myself and my wife, Sarah, about the realization that I had lost my true self—in other words, I was ontologically fractured. Within the constant negotiation between my true self and my social self, I had essentially submitted to the demands and public rewards of ego that I had allowed to remain propped up by my social standing, while at the same time starving my true self. This in turn allowed me to create an unsustainable ego that would eventually cause me to crash and wake up realizing I had been living a perception of the self founded on an illusion.[1] This false self was founded on the illusion of strength, and God was waking me up to the reality that my true self rests solidly on a foundation of weakness.

When we reach the realization or come to the point we are willing to admit that the image we've been portraying is an illusion, we begin to feel the freedom, daunting though it may be, to admit we are living out a story that has been written for us by someone or something else—an institution, culture, society, family of origin, religion, or even the American dream. Typically, our addiction or commitment to this illusion is based on highly esteemed cultural values that never deliver the inner peace we desire. To live in the illusion allows us to deny or ignore the truths about ourselves and our place in the universe which we are convinced are ignoble or a detriment to real life, based on the social track we buy in to. When, in reality, the very truths we often seek to repress or avoid through the illusion are the very truths that allow us to live the unique expression of our humanity in our particular now. In short, strength, if we can define it that way, was not making me a better person, but was deceptively protecting me from becoming who God was shaping me to be.

It wasn't until the apostle Paul embraced weakness, an attribute or value that his culture, as well as ours, taught him to be ashamed of, that he began to live out the unique expression of the Christ life that he was meant to live. And it wasn't until he realized his "thorn in the flesh" was not a handicap or disposition in need of remedy, but rather God's gift that allowed

---

1. Rollins, *Idolatry of God*, 54. By "ego" I am referring to the false image I had of myself, that I presented on a daily basis through work, recreation, and social media.

him to live in the freedom and peace of God's limitless grace.[2] My point is this: the unquestioned social narratives that we assume as normative are built on a set of values that both promote and establish an agenda that often runs contrary to the kingdom narrative of God, and thus our place in that narrative. If the agenda itself is contrary to the one we intimately long for at a subconscious level, then it goes without saying that the values that support the common social narrative are also contrary to the values that support the kingdom narrative. When we live into the values contrary to the those threaded throughout the kingdom narrative, we slowly become a shadow of our true self. This brings us to a fork in the road in our own journey: We can either fit into the cultural definition of normal by committing to the social agenda of our era and context embodied in the institutions, religions, and entertainment of our day, or we take the road less traveled, constantly deal with living outside of that which has been deemed normal, often times without any tangible benefits to validate our choice to live by an alternative narrative. In a society guided by instant gratification, it is easy to understand why the majority of us will settle for normal.

I believe this is how strength becomes the guiding value that actually protects us from who we were divinely created to be. It is like a schizophrenic relationship between the kingdom of God and our own little kingdoms of self. The kingdom of self is sustained and built on a foundation of values propagated by the social agenda, which is often embodied in the institutions, religions, politics, and entertainment of our day. More times than not, especially in a consumer-based society that has, in the church, wedded itself to moralistic deism, these values run counter to the values of Jesus' kingdom. To this Jesus says, "You can't serve two masters," and the God of the Hebrews continually warned his people against idolatry.[3] We can't do it. I literally mean we cannot do it, as in we don't have the ability to do it. I'm not saying we shouldn't do it, I literally mean we are incapable of doing it. This is where strength comes in. Because while we do not have the ability to sustain the kingdom of self in conjunction with the kingdom of God, we are attracted to both.[4] The problem is that both are competing narratives. So we have to rely on our "strength" and ability to override what Jesus says we can't do. We have to use our will, grit, and strength to blend these two narratives together. But the narratives are stronger than

2. 2 Corinthians 12:7–11.

3. Matthew 6:24; Deuteronomy 13.

4. Romans 7.

us. Eventually one wins out. If our affections are turned more deeply toward the narrative that is influenced and influences the kingdom of self, we typically get to stay with our illusion of strength, as we slowly and often times unknowably loosen our grip on the kingdom of God and settle into the kingdom of self. After all, it is more appealing and it does, if only momentarily, feel really good to be the hero of our own story.

The kingdom of God will not allow this. In order to fully embrace and enter into the kingdom of God as our lived reality, we have to come to the end of ourselves. We have to recognize who we are not, just as much as we have to recognize who we are. To do this, we must begin with admitting, embracing, and settling into weakness.

Once we admit, embrace, and settle into weakness, we are finally postured to experience the Divine.[5] We are finally open to the life that the Spirit desires to live through us. Weakness is the ultimate context through which the true self is birthed.[6] To embrace weakness is not to deny power, rather it is to begin to acknowledge where the power to live the life we were called to live resides. It is to admit who wields the power, and subsequently who doesn't. This equation runs throughout the whole of Scripture: weakness as the place where real life begins. It is in the place of weakness, or "dust and ash," where Job comes to know God for who he truly is.[7] It is the place where Jesus unleashes the kingdom.[8] It is where Moses is most ready to be used by God against the powerful of this world.[9] It is where the trajectory of David's life is set in motion.[10] And while the list could go on, there is probably no better story of the juxtaposition between the result of leaning into our own illusion of strength versus submitting to God's strength through our weakness than the story of Samson.[11] But enough of the examples.

It is not lost on me that some of my readers have experienced weakness, and weakness has made you ashamed of who you are: you have not been able to stand up for yourself, for your family, for the oppressed, or for those in need. This has brought you shame. Some of you have connected

5. 2 Corinthians 12:9–10.

6. John 3:1–4.

7. Job 42:1–6.

8. 1 Corinthians 1:17–19.

9. Exodus 4:10-12, 6:28–30.

10. 1 Samuel 17.

11. Judges 13–16.

failure, insecurity, or low-self-esteem with weakness, and therefore committing to weakness almost sounds psychologically abusive. Some of you desire, at least on the surface, to be risk-takers in life, but up to this point, in actuality, you shrink back from being the risk-taker you long to be—vocationally, physically, and/or narratively—and in a way have categorized yourself as weak due to the paralyzation brought on by the idea of risk. So, to claim weakness for you is more of a life sentence in the prison of self-hatred, as opposed to the freedom to live within the power of God and his kingdom. While I have much to say about risk-taking, standing up for yourself and others, and low-self-esteem, these do not fall under the ideal of the weakness I am writing about. In what follows, I will spend a brief time writing about what I actually mean when I talk of weakness as a value. Then I will close out this chapter by discussing how I found contentment within the framework of weakness.

The difficulty of discussing or enacting weakness comes with the fact that there doesn't seem to be any real tangibility to this concept. If you are like me, you may have assigned the ideal of weakness into the heady realm of a philosophical idea that one cannot really act upon. There doesn't seem to be any real tangibility to this concept. I take much delight in things like concepts and theory, maybe because, while I am learning to love the tactile, I still find my home in the academic realm. However, by profession, I am not an academic. I am a practitioner. My hands are dirty. When I speak of theory and practice, I am not reflecting back on an internship or field work I did a decade ago that still informs the theory I have learned to argue well. Therefore, when I work on a theory, I, at the same time attempt to bring the ethereal into the concrete. For me, weakness takes on flesh when I commit to leading my life through the path of submission. Submission to process. A process that I do not dictate, rush, or manipulate, rather a process that molds me.

Submission

The key to abiding in weakness begins with the willingness to live into submission. On one hand, I realize many of you have been bullied into submission by religious zealots twisting Scripture to "submit" to an abusive boss, husband, pastor, or belief system. For that I am sorry. God has not called you into abuse. What these bullies hope that you never find out is that true submission to God will often look like rebellion against those who, in the name of God, keep you from being your real self. Some of you need to leave your current situation—you need to rebel in the name of submission.

I am becoming more convinced that the idea of submission has become taboo, not so much because we hate authority (though there is truth to this), rather because we hate limits. We've been told since we were very young that we can do whatever we want, the world is ours, our horizons are limitless, or the latest phrase, "You can have it all." We have been told that the only thing that holds us back in life is ourselves (this is often true as well). If we can dream it, we can do it. Most of us reading this have lived long enough to know that isn't true. What we have found is that falsity behind the "You can do anything you want" theory doesn't lie so much with ability or the lack thereof, but has much more to do with priority and capacity. In a "You can have it all" world, capacity loudly screams, "No you can't." And priority accompanies that message by saying, "And that's okay." In fact, our culture has ignored the limits of capacity that refuses to accept the proof of its necessity by denying the rise of stress, heart disease, high blood pressure, obesity, depression, suicide, and more. Which is ironic, isn't it? We want to deny capacity because we foolishly believe we can "have it all," that there is no such thing as enough, and yet in denying capacity to prove we can "have it all" we have created cultural, physical, emotional, and mental ailments that end up preventing us from living in the joy we could have had by submitting to contentment. In other words, our drive to "have it all" often results in having less than we could have had we submitted to the reality of capacity.

Submission is simply the acknowledgment of capacity as a reality. To acknowledge the existence of capacity we are then forced to accept the truth that there are consequences to pushing beyond that capacity. Some of those consequences have bettered humanity. Some, and many would argue more, have been toward our detriment. We live in a universe that has natural laws, and a world that has natural, moral, and man-made laws. Those laws, when broken, have both man-made and natural consequences. By submitting to capacity, we are not denying that boundaries can't or sometimes shouldn't be pushed. They can, and as a species we will continue to do so. I am not proposing we stop every time we see a boundary in our way. Not at all. What I am proposing is that we slow down enough to pay attention to the cost at which we are trying to move beyond our capacity—both socially and personally. I am suggesting, before we attempt to move beyond our capacity, we take note of the human cost—to those around us and our self. Often times the correct response when it comes to stretching the limit of our capacity rarely falls on the extreme "yes" or "no," but rather, it falls somewhere in the middle, and requires a slower, more thoughtful movement forward that both makes room for progress while protecting the hearts of those who would have been adversely affected had we simply charged through the walls of our capacity. Everything we do has consequence, and when we submit to that reality, we begin to center ourselves into a worldview that takes into account the chain reactions set off by our decisions.

Our lack of submission to or even belief in our own capacity has caused such an upswing in our loneliness, which has lead to our rise in anxiety, depression, and more. The truth is, submitting to capacity has the potential to lead us into deep community. Submitting to capacity and process allows one to release the chains of drivenness in order to enjoy the now. The idea of living for tomorrow is an ideal so pervasive in our culture that pausing to enjoy the now is often lumped in with idea of laziness and lack of vision. We believe that one day will be better than now; it will be more satisfying and fulfilling if we take everything we are plus some and throw it into that thing—job, vision, ministry, that (you fill in the blank), yet when we do that, as I've mentioned above, we are left feeling like we haven't done enough. The remedy? Throw more into it. Invest more time. Sacrifice the little we have left over to achieve that very evasive tomorrow.

I know people whose resumes impresses the best of us, and can run businesses like those in the best business magazines, but are losing their friends, communities, sons, daughters, and spouses. I know couples who, after twenty years of marriage, come to the realization after the kids have left home that they don't know each other. I have friends, who at the age of thirty, forty, or fifty are at the doctor's office getting blood pressure meds filled because they can't keep up with the demands of life in faith that there is light at the end this tunnel they are traveling down. These are all issues of capacity. We, for some reason, are insecure about our capacity. When capacity can be a place of rest and health, we treat it like an enemy.

The other day one of my son's teammates was telling me he has a stress fracture in the growth plate of his foot. In other words, he has met his capacity. Mind you, he is twelve. He's also one of the quickest kids in the state. He wins every competition he's in. He adds more points to the team than any other single athlete. I've never seen a kid perform like this. I asked him, "Why don't you stop, at least rest? Let your body heal?" His response, "I can't. I can't do that to my team and I can't let go of all I've worked for and accomplished." Except one day he may be forced to. Every single parent standing around us responded by saying, "I love his attitude, he's amazing." What is wrong with our society? The kid is twelve, for God's sake. Are you kidding me? Recognizing and submitting to our capacity doesn't make one a failure, it makes one human. Listening and submitting to our capacity could be the very thing that saves marriages, ministries, kids, jobs, homes, integrity, and lives. Submitting to capacity may be the very key needed to unlock the life we've always wanted to live. If all I have is now, if all you have is now, why wait for tomorrow? If you can't have it all, why try? Stop. If energy and capacity dance together in this zero-sum game, why not point your energy to what matters and to the life you've always wanted to live? Oh, but let me warn you, if you begin to live the life you've wanted to live, you will fail. It is going to happen. But when you submit to capacity your failures don't define you, in fact, failures are expected and even welcomed. We embrace them like we do the old sage teaching us valuable lessons. Submitting to capacity gives us permission to fail, as well as laugh at those very failures as we move forward with joy rather than a self-inflicted oppression because we haven't achieved a tomorrow that always seems a bit further away than arm's length.

Decentering in Order to Find Your Center

Submitting to capacity and process gives a broader view of the world around us, and helps us accept that we are no longer the center. This is often harder than we assume it will be. Cognitively we all know that we are not the center. On a universal level we know that all revolves around our sun, not us. While we have been trained this fact from a very young age, psychologically we have listened to another message. From a very young age we have, philosophically speaking, been the center. As a baby and toddler, our families center in around us. We can only see through our own eyes. We can only feel our own feelings. Thus most of the decisions we make in life are motivated by how we see and feel it. We read books that only confirm what we already think. We surround ourselves with people who see life the same way we do and agree with many of our assertions about reality. All of this creates a psychological view that believes the world truly does revolve around us. To break from the center is to be intentional. And in our society of self-indulgent, emotionally supported narcissism, to break from the center seems as offensive as self-abuse. Despite the messages we have received and subconsciously agreed with from a very young age, we must decenter.

The necessity of decentering became clearer to me through a two-month road trip that my family and I embarked on as a way to tangibly express our entry into the place of liminality (this journey could make for its own book). Everyone picked a book that they believed would speak to them personally. The book I chose was *Zen and the Art of Motorcycle Maintenance*. In the book, the narrator, quoting Einstein, states, "Man tries to make for himself in the fashion that suits him best a simplified and intelligible picture of the world. He then tries to some extent to substitute the cosmos of his for the world of experience, and thus to overcome it . . . He makes this cosmos and its construction the pivot of his emotional life in order to find in this way the peace and serenity which he cannot find in the narrow whirlpool of personal experience . . . There is no logical path to this . . . Only intuition, resting on sympathetic understanding of experience can reach them." I have no doubt that in all my accomplishing and drivenness, I was simply seeking peace, joy, and serenity. The world I was beginning to leave was a world I had constructed to find peace, joy, and serenity. The irony to this was the world I had constructed was more like a bunker that protected me from the peace, joy, and serenity I'm actually seeking. This is why the journey of liminality is necessary. We must intentionally engage a journey that continually reminds us that we are not in control, we are not the center, and everything we construct based on self-glorification will eventually end in disaster. The narrator continues to make his point:

> . . . that kind of motivation (ego goals) is destructive. Any effort that has self-glorification as its final endpoint is bound to end in disaster . . . when you try to climb a mountain to prove how big you are, you almost never make it. And even if you do it's a hollow victory. In order to sustain the victory you have to prove yourself again and again, driven forever to fill a false image, haunted by the fear that the image is not true and someone will find out. That's never the way![12]

I cannot tell you how many times in my ministry career I told Sarah, "I feel like a fake." I had been living according to ego, without realizing it. The quantifying of number goals, the locker-room-type comparisons among pastors of accolades, name dropping, book deals, etc. all seem to

---

12. Pirsig, *Zen and the Art of Motorcycle Maintenance*, 189.

make it impossible to function outside of the ego realm. And rather than change it we find a way to cover it up with spiritualities, religious jargon, and platform stewardship, completely deceived that we are functioning according to God's Spirit. We've all been here. We know what it is like to be the emperor with no clothes. We know what it is like to appear like a confident professional all the while feeling like a fake. The narrator will continue with a parable to drive the point home:

> . . . he (a man on a holy pilgrimage) never reached the mountain.
> After the third day he gave up exhausted, and the pilgrimage went
> on without him. He said he had the physical strength but that physical strength wasn't enough. He had the intellectual motivation but
> that wasn't enough either. He didn't think he had been arrogant but
> thought that he was undertaking the pilgrimage to broaden his experience, to gain understanding for himself. He was trying to use
> the pilgrimage for his own purposes and gains. He regarded himself
> as the fixed entity, not the pilgrimage or the aim, and thus wasn't
> ready for it. He speculated that the other pilgrims, the ones who
> reached the mountain, probably sensed the holiness of the mountain so intensely that each footstep was an act of devotion, an act
> of submission to the holiness. The holiness of the act of submission
> to this holiness of the pilgrimage. The holiness of the mountain infused into their own spirits enabled them to endure far more than
> anything he, with his greater physical strength could take.[13]

So many of us, leaders, pastors, business owners, parents, seem to believe we are the "fixed entity." We believe we exist to shape the pilgrimage, the sabbatical, the church, etc., when the truth is, it is the Spirit within those things that shape us—we are part of an ecosystem that is bigger than us, we are not the fixed entity. However, and this is why intentionality is key, everything in the way we are trained and motivated says otherwise. I started this pilgrimage out much like the man on the holy journey mentioned above, "trying to use the pilgrimage for" my "own purposes." I "regarded" myself "as the fixed entity, not the pilgrimage or the aim." This thinking is natural to me, it's part of the "calling" mantra here in the Western church, we're brainwashed with it. Without even thinking about it, I believe when I enter a scenario it's because I am being called to change it, which is another way of stating that I believe "I'm the fixed entity." The narrator continues:

13. Pirsig, *Zen and the Art of Motorcycle Maintenance*, 189.

To the untrained eye ego-climbing and the selfless climber may appear identical. Both kinds of climber places one foot in front of the other. Both breathe in and out at the same rate. Both stop when tired. Both go forward when rested. But what a difference! The ego-climber is like an instrument that's out of adjustment. He puts his foot down an instant too soon or too late. He is likely to miss a beautiful passage of sunlight through the trees. He goes on when the sloppiness of his step shows he is tired. He rests at odd times. He looks up the trail trying to see what's ahead even when he knows what's ahead because he just looked a second before. He goes too fast or too slow for the conditions and when he talks his talk is forever about somewhere else, something else. He is here but he's not here. He rejects the here, is unhappy with it, wants to be further up on the trail but when he gets fixed there, he will be just as unhappy because then it will be "here." Every steps an effort both physically and spiritually because he imagines his goal to be external and distant.[14]

There are three truths I was able to mine from these readings from *Zen and the Art of Motorcycle Maintenance* that make the journey of liminality possible. The first is that I am not the "fixed entity." It is God. Not the god created in my image, but the God that I barely know. The God who loves me enough to allow my conquests motivated by drivenness to leave me emptier than I was before I began. The second truth I came to believe is that the place, the pilgrimage, the sabbatical, the church is not there for me to change, rather I am invited into these places to meet and be changed by the God who has hidden himself within them. But the truth that has been hardest for me, as someone who has lived off of fighting against it, is the truth of submission. Submitting to, not fighting against, the very entities that I need to submit to, is where transformation begins to happen.

---

14. Pirsig, *Zen and the Art of Motorcycle Maintenance*, 189.

Interlude: **Cultivating the Liminal Process**

"In the middle of the journey of our life I found myself within a dark woods where the straight way was lost."

—DANTE ALIGHIERI, *INFERNO*

When the fog caused by the explosive act of decentering begins to clear, we have three options. The first, and often most traveled, is to attempt, with everything in us, to swim back to the shore we have left. Almost like the abused returning to the abuser, while we know this path leads us to trauma and burnout, it is familiar, and there is comfort in the familiar. It is much easier to fool oneself into believing we can change this avenue into something better. Plus, at our age, adventuring into new and unfamiliar territories is too scary and goes against the way we have come to understand the story line referred to as "responsibility."

The next most traveled path is to take the first exit we can find on this back road we are calling liminality. This is a typical response that is lead by an emotional hybrid of panic and security. On the road of liminality security seems to constantly evade us. In the West, security is the goal we are all taught to seek out. When the realization that security is no longer in site, we panic, and take the first option that comes our way. While this removes us from the pathway of liminality, it also and often invites us to settle for a life less adventurous than the life we had left, and demands we become the shadow of the person we could be all in the name of immediate security. We've all seen this. We've talked to a parent, grandparent, or new friend, and we hear stories of a previous life that seems so alien to the person they are now. We think, "What happened?" What happened is that when they found themselves on the pathway of liminality, they panicked, because their equation for the successful and secure life didn't work out, and they settled for existence just so they could get off the unpredictable liminal path.

The third option, the one less traveled, is the embracing of liminality as we move forward into the fog. While I felt very lost, it was the latter option that appealed to me. To take the road most traveled seemed the most insane. I actually believe this is the way we have defined insanity in our culture: doing the same thing while expecting different results. I knew how I had arrived in this place of lostness, and it didn't make sense to go back if everything about the universe and the world around me told me life was about becoming and moving forward. Going back didn't seem like an option. The second option seemed none the wiser—I have seen many casualties from this attempt to live a less fulfilling life, and I certainly did not want myself nor my family to be one of them. I would rather try this less traveled road and regret it than settle for safety and live the rest of my days wondering, "What if?" That would be torture. So, as a family we decided to move forward. We decided to embrace this journey of liminality no matter how far the fog stretched. It was time to allow myself to be formed and moved by a vision of beauty and truth, rather than who and what I didn't want to become. And if that meant living in the valley of the unknown for a season, then so be it.

Often times in life it seems the answer to the questions, reveals itself just after we feel we can't take it anymore, just after we move beyond the temptation to take the quick exit. This is what happened for us. Our "exit" opportunities seemed amazing. Opportunities that I have at times, and sometimes still do, wonder if it would have been a better option. I was in Portland and talking with Mary Kate Morse and giving her a summarized version of where I was in life, and she pointed me to an author, Laurence Gonzales. I devoured the book she had recommended, *Deep Survival*. This book did so much for me in the way of surviving this part of my life. However, I think this recommendation was more divine than I had realized in that moment. I did what many do when they find an author they learn to really appreciate. I sought out other books they had written, and that's when I came across Gonzales's book *Surviving Survival*, and this book became my second bible through this season. The title alone gave me confidence. We had survived the initial trauma that resulted in a diagnosis of high-functioning depression with PTSD symptoms. I was no longer on an emotional roller coaster, and now we had to survive this new landscape. Landscapes are made up of various elements. From my house in Austin, my landscape was a backdrop of urban housing and an ever-growing skyline. Many landscape paintings are of wheat fields divided by a smooth stream or small villages in front of gorgeous mountains. My new landscape was about geography, occupation (or lack of), and population.

Surviving Survival is all about resilience theory. Gonzales uses real-life events and stories to lead the reader through the ideas of resilience and how they apply in physically traumatic situations and can be translated into the realm of the emotional and even soulish parts of life. For the next several years, I would study resilience theory anytime I was not devoting my time to the study of theology.

Within my studies I came upon a TED Global talk by Jane McGonigal that divided resilience theory into four realms: physical, mental, emotional, and social.[1] As I look back at my journey, I see how my own resilience took shape through these different realms converging into holistic development and healing. Thus, I will use these four realms referred to by McGonigal for the final chapters of this book. I will rely on Gonzales's work and my personal experiences to talk about how I navigated each realm, creating a holistic framework for the resilience needed at that time, along with an intentional commitment to strengthening resilience in the form of a reserve that would allow me to be more ready for any sort of trauma that I may (and have) face in the future.

Before we begin talking about these four realms, allow me for a moment to refer back to the point in McGonigal's TED talk that inspired me to shape and/or see my own personal development in light of resilience theory. At the beginning of McGonigal's talk she refers to a study conducted by hospice workers.[2] This video caught my attention because I could see I was headed to the same place these that were surveyed had arrived on their deathbed. According to the study McGonigal cites, the top five deathbed regrets are:

1. I wish I hadn't worked so hard.
2. I wish I would have stayed in touch with my friends.
3. I wish I would have let myself be happier.
4. I wish I would have had the courage to express my true self.
5. I wish I would have lived a life true to my dreams instead of what other expected of me.[3]

1. McGonigal, "Game that Can Give You 10 Extra Years."
2. McGonigal, *Super Better*, 6.
3. McGonigal, *Super Better*, 6.

As mentioned above, McGonigal is not the only one pontificating these truths. Simply do a quick Google search about top regrets of the dying, and you will get some version of the list above. For me the scariest part of this was that these each defined my current path. I had bought into the same lie so many other good, hard-working Americans had bought in to. All of this can be summed up in living for the "promise of tomorrow." Meaning, if I work hard enough, then one day I won't have to work so much; one day I will be able to circle back with my friends and family after I have spent the necessary time accomplishing that idealized social status; one day I can let myself be happy, but for now I have to buckle down and earn, do, and accomplish; one day there will be time to live out of my true self, but my true self won't earn the status or income I idolize; one day I won't have as much responsibility and I can go after my dreams. The problem with that is one day never seems to come, and like the stats seem to prophecy, we end up regretting that we didn't make one day happen now! I had effectively and convincingly bought into the lie of "one day."

In chapter 1 of this book I refer to a turning point that came from the book of Ecclesiastes, specifically verse 7:2, which says, "It is better to go to the house of mourning than to the house of feasting; for this is the end of everyone, and the living will lay it to heart." Another way to say this is that if we want to live the life we desire at a deep soul level, then listen to the dying, not those selling a social, corporate, or national agenda. And here it was, in scientific data form. We don't have to guess—we know what is being said in the "house of mourning".

Living in submission to the top five regrets as if they were worthy goals sent me for a tailspin that landed me in deep depression. I spent the first half of this book detailing that journey and the genesis of a new awakening. What the "house of mourning" was telling me was that I can't go back to the "house of feasting" or I will end up just like I had before. So, how was I to dig myself out of this new place of trauma?

As I continued to study resilience theory and as McGonigal confirms, I kept coming across traits of those who not only came through trauma, but thrived after it. The terminology for this is "post-traumatic growth." According to McGonigal, post-traumatic growth happens when we allow traumatic—emotional or physical—events to be a catalyst that launches us into a life of fulfillment and purpose.[4] Here's the deal: there is no neutrality. At this point in life, we either use the trauma to allow ourselves to shrink

---

4. McGonigal, *Super Better*, 8.

and become a shell of the person we were meant to be, or we use it as an engine to thrust us into the self we have always wanted to be. What is so fascinating to me is that those who were intentional in growing through the trauma or who were experiencing post-traumatic growth said they began to experience and give themselves permission to change their priorities, and in doing this they began to focus on doing the things that brought true joy and fulfilment (remember the three questions I asked at the beginning of the book?). They began to grow closer to friends and family; they went on a journey of self-discovery; they gained a new sense of meaning and purpose in life, and began to find an ability to better focus on their dreams over and above the narrative culture tells us we should settle for. In other words, these top five traits of post-traumatic growth are the exact opposite to the top five deathbed regrets. Somehow, if directed correctly, trauma can help us unlock our ability to live fuller and better lives.

Ideally, we all would have listened to the "house of mourning" rather than the "house of feasting" as to avoid this; but let's face it, marketing and the mantra of the American dream makes the "house of feasting" so damn appealing. But for those of us who have traveled down the road of liminality, we know better. Most of us have figured out, and figured out the hard way, we were wrong. So, for those of us who are in the middle of this, or have at the very least been able to gain some sort of calmness about our life, we need practices or rhythms that help us live into these top five traits experienced by those in post-traumatic growth; and for those who have not reached this point in life, maybe, unlike the rest of us, you can put practices in your life that might help prevent you from this sort of trauma.

So, the obvious question is, "How does one intentionally get from trauma to growth?" or "How does one leave this current cultural narrative that has landed so many of us in a state of trauma and depression for a path of fulfillment and purpose?" According to McGonigal there are four kinds of resilience that contribute to post-traumatic growth: physical, mental, emotional, and social.[5]

Throughout the rest of the book I will dedicate one chapter to each aspect of resilience. Within each chapter I will describe each aspect, talk about practices I personally put into play, and suggest some others. Let me remind you, this is not just for of us who have been through this. I believe, ultimately, these can be adapted to any life as a form of holistic discipleship shaping us into humans that better reflect the image of the Divine here on earth. If we

5. McGonigal, *Super Better*, 8.

can apply these as a way of life, and actually learn from the "house of mourning," we will not enter the "house of mourning" with these same regrets the majority of our population does. Before we begin to talk about the realms of resilience, first a word about the most addictive drug in our society—denial.

Denial

As I sat down to write this section, I was doing my equivalent of small talk before I dig deep—I was thumbing through Facebook. I came upon a post by an old acquaintance that said something to the effect of, "This is what self-care looks like today." I scrolled down a little further, and there is a picture of him on some sort of medical ventilator and a story of him being rushed to the hospital for stress-induced chest pains. That is not self-care. That is denial. That is the wake-up call that one needs to begin taking self-care seriously before denial leads them to an early grave. Our society seems to believe that if you just say something is so, it makes it so. When your over-adrenalized, over-worked life leads you to the point you need to be rushed to the hospital due to stress-related chest pains, you cannot simply call that "self-help." This is the point where denial becomes very dangerous.

As a whole, our society is committed to denial as if it were a value. It seems rather than dealing with short-comings, capacity, and failures, we would rather deny it. Our denial comes in many forms. Sometimes it is absolutely verbal. Other times our denial looks like burying ourselves in our work. It seems our denial is medicated through prescription drugs so that we are allowed to ignore the deeper issues going on within us.

While I was not medicating myself with prescription drugs, I was hiding behind my work as a way to deny the breakdown that was happening, to avoid squeaking out the weakness mantra, "I can't handle it anymore." It wasn't so much that I couldn't say those words as I was afraid to admit what those words may be saying about me. I knew other pastors seemed to handle it. In fact, the argument I would have time and time again in my head was, "When I put it all on paper, I should be able to handle it." Paper is deceptive. Paper is doesn't take into account the emotional and mental weight. It doesn't take into other situations that may take a toll on you. It doesn't take into account the fact that you only had three hours of sleep the night before. While paper is good for planning, it is not always the best for evaluating a three-dimensional life. But I couldn't allow myself to believe this. I was in denial. Then physical symptoms began to expose the truth—passing out, gaining weight, and losing extreme weight. I had leaders speaking truth to me, but at the end of the day, denial was my hiding place.

I think this is why it seems to be the drug of choice for our culture; we are afraid of what the truth says about us. We are afraid of the fact that we can't have it all. We are afraid that we can't keep up with the American dream—whatever that is. We are afraid we will never measure up to the idealistic vision in our head. So we deny the truths, symptoms, and voices around us and we keep pushing ourselves.

In *Deep Survival*, Laurence Gonzales goes into several examples of those who make it out alive when they are stranded and lost, and those who don't. He basically says that, for some reason, one group of people refuses to believe they are literally lost. They refuse to believe that this may be it, that this new place of stranded may be their new reality. In refusing to believe this, or in denying their own reality, they foolishly rely on their own strength to immediately attempt to navigate a land they have never been to, and actually end up exhausting their physical and psychological resources only to become more lost than they were in the first place. Gonzales says the first rule of life is: be here now.[6] For a culture like ours this almost seems counterintuitive. We want to ignore our reality and be in the future, live as if our breakdown isn't real, until, like those physically stranded, we exhaust our physical and psychological resources and end up more lost than we were before. Rather, the only way out, the only way through the liminal process is to be right where you are. To admit the deficiency. Admit the shortcoming. Admit the mental breakdown. Admit the depression. Say it. Name it. Not as an excuse, but as a reality check, as a starting point. If we don't start from reality, we will never get on the right track.

Elsewhere Gonzales will say, after we have come to the place of being in reality, or being here now, we must perceive and believe, embrace our current reality, embrace the pain and truth, and then and only then does the world begin to open up to you. We must perceive and believe the truth.[7]

Once we open ourself up to the truth of our reality, it is time to commit to a process that leads us to our tomorrow. In fact, survival is often dependent on our ability to commit and organize our lives around organized processes.[8] This leads us to the second half of the book: the process of resilience.

6. Ganzales, *Deep Survival*, 169.

7. Gonzales, *Surviving Survival*, 39.

8. Gonzales, *Surviving Survival*, 39.

Part 2: **The Journey of Resilience!**

The journey between what you once were and who you are now becoming is where the dance of life really takes place.

—*Barbara De Angelis*

To get through the hardest journey we need take only one step at a time, but we must keep on stepping.

—*Chinese proverb*

Chapter 6: **Physical Resilience**

The secure sense of self is tied up within our bodies . . .
when the body is radically changed so is the self.

—Laurence Gonzales

O ur society has willingly displaced itself by becoming more and more virtual. Much of the Western world does work that is virtual in some sense, and thus not located in a place. The more our society becomes uprooted from the physical landscapes and places that we used to call home in order to live in the ethereal, virtual world, the more we will experience increased movement toward social depression, anxiety, and lostness. If this is true for our society, this is true for us as individuals. Bad memories and experienced traumas happened within and to our bodies. Our good memories, and most joyful experiences, happened in and to our bodies. Any remedy or aim at developing resilience that does not begin in the physical body will never allow us to truly begin the journey to wholeness. According to Jane McGonigal, when developing resilience the number one thing you can commit to is physical movement. Avoid sitting still. Be physical. Every second you are not sitting still you are improving the muscular and cellular resilience of your body, which, as we will see, transcends through all the other aspects of resilience. The gateway to reviving your soul is to begin squarely planted in your body.

There are two quotes that apply deeply to this. Unfortunately, I don't know where the quotes originated so I can't give credit to anyone specifically. What I can say is that, like a mantra, I've heard these phrases time and time again in family life, the church world, and the business realm. One of the quotes goes like this: "Sometimes we have to act our way into a feeling." And the other is, "Feelings are awful leaders, but good followers."

I want to be clear about one thing before we begin to talk about the physicality to developing resilience, and that is, I am not anti-feelings. There are many times in life we should listen to our feelings (and many times that we shouldn't). Feelings make our experiences deeper—just for a moment think about the first time you met your newborn child. Or when you stood across from your spouse at the altar. The first time you took that job you were longing for. Or the time you lost your first love. That time you were betrayed by the person you trusted most. Yeah, you get it. The list could go on. Feelings make our experiences that much richer and weightier. So, if you get lost in this chapter and begin to believe that I am writing off feelings, return to this paragraph. I am not. However, there are negative things we can say about feelings, and those usually have to do with feelings outside of accountability. The truth is, most people who have gotten themselves in deep financial trouble, who have cheated on their significant other, who have made really bad life choices, have done so because at the root of those decisions lies an emotion or feeling that tells us this will be a good choice, this will make us happier, or this is what we really want. This is the first sin recorded in the Bible. The serpent plays to their emotions and feelings, and everything goes poorly and the rest of humanity continues to follow this same pattern.

When it comes to the need to develop resilience due to a physical, spiritual, or emotional trauma, emotions, at least initially, will not lead us in the right direction. Sometimes our emotions will paralyze us with fear. Sometimes they will, if given the right to lead, lead us onto a more destructive path. More than anything, they will lead us into a state of confusion simply due to the fact they are changing all the time. And when decisions are being dictated by ever changing emotions, we end up living a schizophrenic existence at best, or worst case we end up stuck, unable to move due to fear of what else could happen.

For me, my emotions, depending on the day, would tell me I am a fake, I am a failure, I should hate myself, I am going to wreck my family, and worst, I should die to relieve everyone else of all they have to suffer because of my existence. Other days my emotions tried to argue in a very convincing manner that I should just leave it all, including my family. My emotions would say, "Yes, they will hurt at first, but the hurt is an illusion; they will see the light and realize their life is better for it." Other times I felt extreme highs, and wanted to take chances that can only be explained as manic. And this is where the phrase "Feelings are awful leaders, but good followers" comes into play.

Had I allowed my feelings to rule, to lead, to guide, I'm not sure I would even be on earth today. I'm pretty sure I wouldn't be married. And I'm certain I would be drowning in regret. This is where that second quote began to take shape in my life: sometimes we have to act our way into a feeling. I had enough wherewithal to know or at least hope that my feelings were wrong and destructive. So, when I didn't feel like being affectionate with Sarah, I made myself. When I didn't want to listen to the kids tell me about their day, I did. When I didn't want to go out with people, I did. When I wanted to allow the cloak of depression to keep me in bed, I got up. In short, I acted against my feelings. At this point, often times I did not have the mental clarity to always know the difference between what I should and shouldn't do, so I had to rely on community—my wife, friends, and family—and basically give them authority over me, specifically my feelings. As I began to choose over and against my ever-changing emotions, I began to find solid footing. I began to realize that while I could not physically change my emotions, feelings, and thoughts, I could control the way I acted. According to Gonzales, the secure sense of self is tied up within our bodies. So, when the body is radically changed so is the self.[1] The body can only be changed through action. So, as we begin to use movement, we begin to change emotion, leading us to a secure sense of who we are, which is what was ultimately lost in our trauma. In other words, what we do with the body forces structure on the mind and this in turn trickles down to our emotional being. The body controls the brain. What we do with the body is going to influence what goes on in the brain, which in turn allows us to naturally alter our emotional state. Active coping, physically redirects the flow of information in the brain and ultimately leaves feelings like fear and depression behind and makes way for us to begin to get on with life.[2]

For me, I couldn't start with big changes. I didn't have it in me. I started with what I have come to call "active contemplation." In 1948 Thomas Merton wrote a small pamphlet entitled "What Is Contemplation?" In this pamphlet he states that contemplation "is spontaneous awe at the sacredness of life, of being. It is a vivid realization of the fact that life and being in us proceed from an invisible, transcendent, and infinitely abundant source. Contemplation is above all, awareness of the reality of that source," which

1. Gonzales, *Surviving Survival*, 55.
2. Gonzales, *Surviving Survival*, 114.

ultimately leads to a more "profound depth of faith, a knowledge too deep to be grasped in images, in words, or even in clear concepts." According to Merton, contemplation is not simply a verb, but it is a state of being. When we are in a state of contemplation, we are, according to Merton, more connected to the Divine, to ultimate reality, and to our true self. For centuries one of the spiritual habits Christians included in their daily disciplines was contemplation as a verb. They would contemplate or enter into "contemplative prayer." Contemplative prayer is a process through prayer in which one stills their thoughts and emotions and focuses on God. The hope is that we grow in our awareness of the Divine by unlearning habits of noise and speed, which have ultimately blocked us from having a true vision of not only God, but of our true self as well. As our hearts grow silent we begin to hear God's voice for our life.[3] In short, contemplative prayer, in the Christian tradition, is the process of silencing the mind in order to become more aware of who God is, the Divine's movement in our world, and who we were created to be. However, my mind was the definition of noise and chaos, as demonstrated in the opening chapter. I could not still my mind, and when I would try, my mind would become a storm of haunting chaos. At this time, since I could not still my mind through contemplation, I enacted what I have come to call active contemplation. The idea behind active contemplation is to physically engage in and submit to a slow, directed process with the aim at arriving in the same place contemplative prayer seeks to arrive.

Since I began active contemplation I have run into other articles about such practices, but at the time I had never heard of it. All I knew was that I needed a slow, directed process that would allow my mind to focus on anything other than the darkness in my head. The key word here is "process." A good friend of mine, Tyler Northcutt, defines process as "an identifiable path one takes in order to bring anything to life." Which is what I needed; I needed to be brought back to life, as did my vision for God, reality, and life. To do this, I had to submit myself to small practices that demanded a process, and that process had to become king. We don't rule the process, the process rules us and we submit.

For me, active contemplation began with two things: sourdough bread baking and beer brewing. That's right, baking bread and brewing beer were my spiritual practices! Why did I choose these? Simple. I like really good bread and delicious craft beer. So, why not learn to make them. I also love to

3. Johnson, *When the Soul Listens.*

be in the kitchen. If I begin to feel anxious, I either need to get outside or get into the kitchen and cook, bake, or brew. To get the bread and beer I wanted I had to submit to a long process. There was no quick fix. I couldn't force the end to come quicker. Well, I suppose there probably are ways to do so, but not with what I wanted the outcome to be. Seriously, as stated above, I needed to reset my emotional and mental state of being, and to do that I implemented a very physical practice that resulted in a very tactile outcome. This demanded that my mind and emotions stay present within a specific process, not unlike paying attention to your breathing as you meditate in the hopes of clearing your mind. If my mind and emotions left the process, what I was doing was ruined, and I had to start over.

Starting over was not something I wanted to do. Sourdough bread and the type of beers I wanted to brew, beers that are more reminiscent of old-world beers, took a long time to produce. Both of them took precise measuring, especially as I began to create my own recipes. For example, it took me two whole weeks to create my sourdough starter. A sourdough starter is essentially the yeast. Up until this point in my life, if I was going to bake bread, I was going to purchase my dried yeast from a grocery store, and it was going to be ready for use within fifteen minutes of activating with some sort of sugar water. Not a sourdough starter. It took me days of "feeding" it with a precise amount of water and flour, keeping it in the proper temperature, allowing it the right amount of oxygen, while keeping foreign bacteria away. Two weeks just to get the yeast I was going to use. Grant it, once you create that starter, you've got it, but you have to continually nurture it to keep it alive. It doesn't end there. It takes me thirty-plus hours to produce a good loaf of bread. I pull my starter out of the fridge and pour eighty grams into a mason jar. I allow it to get to room temperature, and then add a few more hours onto that. I then add the eighty grams of starter to one hundred grams of my flour mix and one hundred grams of water, and depending on the ambient temperatures in the house it takes up to ten hours for the leaven to be produced. Once it is produced, I knead together the different flours and water with the leaven. Then I let it rest for another two to four hours. After that, I add wheat germ, sprouted grains, and salt and allow it to rest from anywhere between three to six hours, making sure I revisit the dough and knead it every thirty minutes for the first two hours of that three-to-six-hour period. Then I move into a shaping period that lasts about thirty minutes, which culminates with the dough being placed into its basket. I cover it and put it in the fridge so that it can cold ferment for about ten hours. After it is finished cold fermenting, it is finally time to turn the cold shaped dough into piping hot loaves of fresh, airy sourdough bread. To do this I have to turn the oven to five hundred degrees, and place my cast iron Dutch oven in the stove until it reaches that temperature and begins to produce steam within the Dutch oven. This waiting takes about twenty minutes. Once the Dutch oven has reached the temperature, I pull a loaf of dough out of the fridge, drop it into the Dutch oven, score the bread, put the lid on, and stick it back in the stove for about forty-five minutes. Then, after a thirty-five-hour process that I have had to stay intimately involved in, I have what I was aiming for . . . kind of. And that's the thing, I can always get better. I can always produce a better crumb or crust. I can always adjust the flavor, but to do this, not only do I have to stay intimately committed to the process, I have to repeat the process time and time again to get a better loaf each time.

This is not a "how to bake bread" or "how to brew beer" book, so I'll leave it there. The reason I even went into the detail I did above was to give you a glimpse of the process that I committed myself to. It wasn't just any process. It was a new, complex process that would not allow my mind to go into autopilot. I had to be present the whole time. In fact, there is science behind this as well. When one first learns a skill such as knitting, baking bread, brewing beer, or even something like camping or riding a bike, it begins as a voluntary, deliberate action that requires conscious thought. According to Gonzales, "when learning a new skill, you have to think about it consciously. You have to make deliberate use of your body, step by step. It won't be smooth. You'll have to work at it. But as you practice control migrates out of the frontal lobes into the lower parts of the brain and the activity becomes automatic. The basal ganglia becomes involved and your movements begin to flow. Your cerebellum and parietal lobe begin to monitor what you're doing and correct errors automatically."[4] In other words, you literally, through a physical process begin to enter and create a new holistic state of being, in which both the emotional and the mental are wrapped up in.

The point being that physical practices that demand submission to process, pattern, repetition, and organization, all directed toward an end goal, have proved to be healing for people suffering from loss, trauma, and/or grief.[5] So, what does beer brewing and bread baking have to do

4. Gonzales, *Surviving Survival*, 110.
5. Gonzales, *Surviving Survival*, 109.

with the spiritual realm? Nothing and everything. They have nothing to do with spiritual shaping in and of themselves, just like wine and bread have nothing to do with the blood and body of Christ on their own. These things are tools that help us refocus our being in the direction they need to go. For bread or beer, or writing, knitting, sewing, wood work, or anything else that forces us to submit to a process to become a spiritual practice, it simply takes intention. No more or no less than meditating, praying, or reading the Bible. It all has to do with the intention behind it and our submission to a process.

My former co-pastor from Church at East talks about how he uses the process of wood working to pray over the families he is crafting furniture for. Once bread baking and beer brewing moved from the awkward clunky phase into more of an automatic flow, so did my mental and emotional direction. All of the sudden I could use the different "stations" of bread baking as ways to direct my thoughts and prayers. For instance, we all know that Scripture isn't lacking on texts about yeast or leaven. So, when I am working on mixing the leaven or yeast into the dough, I am praying that the Spirit will begin to work through me (and others) just as the leaven or yeast is working through the dough. When I am kneading the dough, I am asking the Divine to use the things in my life to "knead" me into the very human I should be. I think you get the point. These seemingly small practices like sewing, wood working, bread baking, or beer brewing have the potential to direct our mind and emotions to a healthier state of being. These practices have the potential, when intention is applied, to open up our entire being to healing and forward movement into realms of health, creativity, and beauty.

On a Communal Level

A family or community is a physical, emotional, and relational system made up of differentiated selves that are not autonomous of the rest of the system members. In short, nothing can happen to or by a member of the family system that does not in some form effect the other members. We are not autonomously independent of the other. Our entire existence and identity is caused by the other members of the system. I realize this goes against American individualism or the thought that the individual is the building block of civilization. But none of us live independently of one another, and if that is true then it is also true with our emotional state as well as the decisions we make. My psychological and emotional state did not just affect me, it affected everyone who was connected to me, especially my family.

If my personal identity was being transformed, so was my family's. My family could not continue to be committed to our former system if the contributions I made as my former or jaded self would no longer be contributed. In other words, the change in me would disrupt the current family system. If I was going to develop or change, so were they. That's never a question. The question is how will they change, for good or for ill. So, we began to ask each other as well as research how we as a family could introduce new hobbies and habits that inject the idea of process into the core of who we are as we begin to better and adapt our system.

We picked up several new practices, none of which are out of the norm from many families. If anything, the element that set these practices apart was not so much the practices themselves but the intention behind them. For many of us, that simple step, pausing and finding or adding the intention behind what we do, could be enough to alter much of the hurriedness and/or anxiety felt within our family units. Once we do this, many of us will discover that some of our practices are actually pointless and no longer need to take up room on our schedules. For others, we may discover the driving force behind some of our practices are not deeper than "doing it because we have always done it." When we come to this realization we have a choice to make: drop the practice, or do a little work and find the original intent behind those practices, and if the intent is still relevant allow that intent to breathe new life into them.

For us, we wanted to institute practices that we had never been involved with, that demanded we use some sort of family-groupthink, to stay committed and present within the process. Our family added two practices, as not to be too overwhelming. We wanted these practices to act as visible and tangible sacraments of something greater than the acts themselves. One of the practices would be something we could do on a regular basis. It required less planning, and gave opportunity to several different members of the family to take lead of the group. It called for perseverance, especially by the younger ones, and the older ones had to grow in patience. And most of all it helped teach us to think as a unit, so those of us who were older and stronger had to always take the younger and physically weaker into consideration. This first practice was long bike rides. The second practice only took place once or twice a year, but it demanded much more planning.

It taught us to see life as a journey, and an adventure, rather than a destination. It is my opinion that living with a "destination mentality" robs us as a culture from fully living in the present. This practice taught us that sometimes the best traveled roads are the ones not planned for. It taught us to find life in the places we often miss it. It taught us that everyone on the team has an important role to play—from the thirty-nine-year-old dad to the seven-year-old daughter. It taught us to contribute according to our ability and only expect to be given according to our need. And it taught us that mass modern acceptance of conventional wisdom doesn't always work. This practice was road-tripping and camping. Again, most any family can adopt these practices, but they only add to the development of physical and ultimately spiritual resilience as we become intentional with the motivation and stay committed to the process, for it is commitment to the tactile process that ultimately begins to shape the elements that need the deepest shaping—emotion, mind, and spirit.

Allow me a page or two to explain how we used road-tripping to actualize our commitment to physical resilience. Before we used road-tripping and camping as a spiritual practice, we had never done so before. That's right—fourteen years of marriage, and we had never been camping. So, how did we know this might work for us? It started with an invitation, a random Facebook post, and the need to get out of my current location. Let me explain. When we lived in Austin we had a pretty amazing network and group of friends. One day I received a call from our friends at Kammok Adventure Gear (our favorite outdoor adventure company) asking us if we wanted to do a video shoot and an overnight primitive camping experience with the famed adventurer Alastair Humphreys. Though I had never been camping before, one does not simply say no to this sort of invitation. So we did it. Long story short, we loved it! We were amazed at how soul-refreshing it was to be out of the city and immersed into nature. No screens, music, or electronics, just nature. It was easy to get a glimpse into the possible and positive long-term effects of being outdoors, never mind all the studies that seem to back this.[6] We had to rely on each other and remain completely interdependent. We had to use instinct. There seemed

6. Examples of studies:
Moore et al., "Global Urbanization and Impact on Health."
Sundquist et al., "Urbanisation and Incidence of Psychosis and Depression."
National Park Service, "Healthy Parks Healthy People."
Mitchell and Popham, "Effect of Exposure to Natural Environment."

to be much about camping in the outdoors that were based on some of the processes found in physical resilience.

The Facebook post that we landed on was a random post entitled, "One Guy Figured Out How to Plan the Best Road Trip Ever."[7] This grabbed my attention, because at this point we were actively seeking out a family adventure that we had never done before. Another reason this piqued our curiosity was that since the beginning of our marriage we had done small road trips—800–1,000 miles—to visit our families for the holidays. In the beginning, the point was never the road trip, it was the destination, but slowly we began to look forward to the road trip just as much as the destinations.

We knew that long-term camping and a very long road trip would demand we create a process that we had to submit to if we wanted the trip to be a journey of restoration and revitalization. To do this, we first assessed the differing abilities of each member. Our youngest was six, and I was thirty-nine—that is a huge age span. Needless to say, we each contributed different abilities and came with different sets of needs. Starting with the six-year-old and moving up the ladder, each person had abilities that those beneath them in age did not have. This being the case, we had to begin with the oldest and strongest of the group, me. What jobs needed to be done that only I could do? Those jobs became mine. Then was Sarah. Then Serena and so on. This allowed us to create a system for setting up tents and campfire cooking as well as finding the right type of kindling to both start and keep the fire going. The first time or two, not unlike bread, were pretty clunky, but by the end of the trip it was pretty seamless. Like a well-oiled system where all the parts equally contribute according to their ability, we ended each night around a fire, with hot food, good stories, and comfortable tents awaiting our bedtime. A process was created. Everyone committed according to their abilities. Everyone's needs were met.

Enacting the Metaphor

Do a casual search, eavesdrop on surrounding conversations and it won't take you long to hear countless voices using the idea of a journey—pilgrimage, trip, road trip, or even hike as a metaphor for life. As mentioned above, the road trip was our metaphor to a new destination, and the process was the metaphor for the way we would live this new life. Standing

7. Ledbetter, "One Guy Figured Out How to Plan the Best Road Trip Ever."

at my vantage point, it is difficult for me not to assign a long road trip to families or communities who are beginning the process of transitioning from one world to another. Through road trips we are literally enacting the metaphor. Road trips are great and frustrating. There are no quick fixes on a road trip. You can't escape the people you are traveling with, and when you have a family the size of mine, someone is always going to mess up your good timing with a bathroom break (to be fair, that person was usually me). But if you are fighting with your spouse, there is no way to ignore it or escape it, because they are sitting right next to you the whole time. Road-tripping is all about tangible vulnerability.

Finally, as I stated, I needed to leave and get out. I had been given the option to take a sabbatical two years before this but did not accept due to how busy we were (which is the exact reason I should have taken it). When given the original opportunity I was already beyond burnout. Now, add two more years of burnout and you reach a fork in the road: explode or leave. These three elements were the perfect storm that motivated our original camping road trip, which lead to shorter subsequent camping road trips since then.

We did it, after that one night camping trip with Alistair Humphreys; we set out for a two-month road trip. We did not stick to the trip found in the *Huffington Post*, but we did use it as a base to build on. We knew we couldn't do the entire United States in two months and enjoy it, but we did eighteen states, including all of the Western states, and boy are they big. One of the best aspects was that we found other organizations with similar values that wanted to help us tell our story and thus sponsored our road trip with in-kind donations (food, clothing, knives, camping gear, and hotels, beer, coffee).[8] The trip started out very chaotic, and the darkest side of my "get it done" personality kicked into full gear the first week of the trip, so much so that I'm pretty sure I sucked the fun out of it for everyone. That's the thing about being committed to something new that demands process; sooner or later it will cause the worst part of you to surrender and submit to the process, which I did. Because of this submission the trip went from chaotic to cathartic. Yes, pilgrimages transform us! The road trip became a metaphor for our life. In fact, since that trip we have repeated it again through the Northeastern quadrant of the United States

8. Special thanks to Kammok, Dark Clan Jiu Jitsu, Weige Knives, La Quinta, GSI Out Doors, Epic Provision, Clif Bars, Cuvee Coffee, Strange Land Brewery, Mitscoots, and Howler Brothers.

and then again in the Mid-Atlantic. In fact, if there is any turmoil in the family and it seems to be deeper than getting up on the wrong side of the bed, we usually pack up and go on a mini road trip as way to reset and remind ourselves of who we are.

At the end of the day, if you are married, it isn't enough to commit yourself to developing physical resilience; you are part of an interdependent tribe, and because of that everything you are going through, they are too. If you are single, still, you are not an autonomous individual despite our cultural mantra. You are both a product and contributor of the community you find yourself in. While the other members of your family or community are not in your specific shoes and can't fully relate to what you are going through, neither can you relate to their perspective, and thus you must include them on the path of physical resilience and the recreation of the self. At the end, no matter how your depression, trauma, or lostness began, the healing begins as we use and engage our bodies to change the structure of the memories and habits that might have kept us trapped into the place of darkness.[9]

9. Gonzales, *Surviving Survival*, 118.

Chapter 7: **Mental Resilience**

"All the furniture of his mind was taken away."

—C.S. Lewis, *The Pilgrim's Regress*

I ended the last chapter by referring to the idea that we most effectively shape our minds and emotions as we engage our bodies. Whether your trauma is physical, mental, emotional, or all of the above, it seems to me, that the darkness that holds us back takes root in the mind and heart. I believe this is why we have to start with the physical and allow it to guide us to the next step, which is committing to mental resilience. Or as my wife, Sarah, would say, engaging the body is the anchor that allows us to pursue mental and emotional resilience.

According to McGonigal in her TED Talk, mental resilience is basically tackling a tiny challenge without giving up. This in turn assists in building the mental capacity and resilience that not only helps you live a better life but allows you to prepare for other unforeseen events in the future. This is not just about getting smarter or putting more information in our brains to outweigh the defeating information that's been stored between our ears. Mental resilience is more about boosting one's willpower in order to develop healthy and new mental processes. In fact, whenever a person is in some sort of crisis, be it health, emotional, physical, mental, or economic, their chances of surviving that crisis drastically increases when they have the mental resolve or willpower to see their future based on what they can dream and imagine as opposed to the negative circumstances that surround them.[1]

Before we get into the practical aspect of mental resilience, I want to talk about the structure of the brain and the part it plays in developing mental resilience. To simplify things, think of our brains as having three

---

1. Friedman, *Failure of Nerve*, 162.

layers as well as several regions, all of which play a vital role in the way we live our lives. The smallest layer of our brain, known as the brainstem and cerebellum, is what we call the reptilian brain. You probably guessed, based off of the name, that this part of the brain dictates or controls the basic functions that are even found in reptiles. This part of the brain is responsible for basically keeping us alive by being responsible for the body's vital functions such as heart rate, body temperature, and breathing, it doesn't help us in our quest for being more human. Another basic life function we can count on the reptilian brain to activate is a symptom we call "fight or flight." While at times this symptom can save our lives, it can also cause us to be pretty compulsive when it senses any sort of danger or threat even if the thing or experience sensed does not actually present a threat. This "fight or flight" sense is all about survival, and this is what will often cause us to panic when we encounter something our brain interprets as dangerous. This is why many people have a very difficult time overcoming and moving beyond trauma. To move beyond our trauma one must take risks, and to risk anything is to chance being hurt or failing again. Once trauma is experienced, the reptilian brain goes on high alert for anything that even slightly resembles the experience that caused the trauma in the first place, and while it may protect us from being hurt the same way again, if we cannot find the willpower to override the induced panic, it will also protect us from living the life we want to live by directing us time and again back to a place of bland, domesticated existence. So, while the reptilian brain may have produced the instinct to allow you to survive the initial trauma, it has to be overridden in order to grow in resilience. Please hear me, when I say "override," I don't mean ignore—that could be dangerous. I mean pay attention to what it is saying, and rather than thoughtlessly panicking or reacting, using the next two layers to guide you.

The next layer, sometimes called the middle brain, or the animal brain, is the limbic brain. According to Gonzales, this is where intuition resides. That intuition that seems to come out of nowhere is actually created. It is created and developed by trial and error and feedback on that trial and error. The limbic brain is where memory, emotions, and motivation reside. This is where everything experiential is etched into our emotional system, including traumatic experiences. For example, when you say you know something, but cannot explain or give language to how you know it, it is because you do know it; you actually have the years of information that cause you to know it, but because it is filed away in your limbic brain, you can't necessarily recall the actual information, all you can do is just know.

Finally, we come to the neocortex part of the brain. This is the largest part of our brains and is what gives us the ability to think logically and give language to those feelings and thoughts that seem to bubble up out of nowhere. So, ideally, it is here where we use our consciousness to make decisions, learn new habits, engage new activities, and build up information in which we practice over and over again with intentionality. At some point, this new learned information or mechanics learned from a new skill or hobby is transferred down to the limbic portion the brain and it becomes part of our "subconscious" as it becomes part of who we are. Think of the time period when you learned to ride a bike. At some point you were using the neocortex portion of your brain to learn the mechanics, to learn the direction the pedals needed to go, or which brake handle effected either the front or back brake. You had to attempt to use all of this information to get the bike to go forward without falling. Which didn't happen for a while. Then what happened? One day you got on the bike, and it all clicked. You didn't have to intentionally put all the pieces together; they just naturally came together. That's because the continual practice and commitment to the process and pattern made it to the limbic part of your brain, and it became part of your hard drive, so to speak. This is why a boxer will hit a bag thousands of time a day; not just to learn how to hit, but rather she needs hitting to become a natural response and action. When I started jiu-jitsu, I may have been one of the worst white belts in the class. None of the techniques where natural to me. Until one day they just were. For me, it seemed like certain techniques and defense moves were so clunky even after weeks of practice until two different things happened: I would take a short break, then typically, as weird as it is, I would dream about the move or I could mentally picture it happening. And then the next time I was on the mats, the different techniques flowed. From the neocortex to the limbic. From clunky, willpowered actions to natural flow. Remember, developing mental resilience is not only about learning new information, it is about developing healthy and new mental processes that will eventually become automatic.

This is why we need to commit to learn new activities, new patterns, and create new paths. According to Gonzales, when we intentionally create new habits, engage in new activities, or learn new information, and then repetitively practice what we've learned, we create a new set of cell assemblies that begin to override the old information that had become embedded to the lower parts of our brain from hurt, grief, betrayal, and loss.[2] Here's the deal: our lives are carved out from the stone of memory, so the only way we begin to change our life is by carving new memories out of and over the old ones that seem to haunt us so deeply.[3]

So, in the way of creating mental resilience you are actually doing two things. You are intentionally disrupting the life and way of being you have been naturally existing on that is embedded in the limbic portion of your brain by intentionally living, practicing, and learning habits and information that are not natural to you. You are literally living out of your neocortex. This is completely frustrating and the very reason so many people opt for what they already know. If you hate failure, buckle up. In essence you are unlearning knowledge the limbic relies on (old patterns, memories, and hurts) by committing to the neocortex with all new practices, experiences, knowledge, and habits, knowing that you are actually loading a new way of being into the limbic. In other words, you are recreating yourself by developing healthy and new mental processes.

Most of the things we can thoughtlessly do in our day-to-day life are part of something called "mental maps." Think of it this way. When you move to a new place, you have to use most of your senses to get where you want to go. There is no autopilot. You have to pay attention to everything, not only to where you are, but to everything you pass—signs, stoplights, building, traffic patterns, new traffic laws, etc. However, something begins to happen the more you make that same route. You begin to be less intentional about the very things you were intentional about just a month before. Then at some point you will go from point A to point Z, all the while thinking about something completely different, and may even have that famous experience where you might say, "I don't even remember driving here." Why is that? You have built a new mental map that allows you to simply go on autopilot and still arrive at the same destination. This doesn't just happen when we drive. Think of jogging routes, social situations, and hobbies. At one point they were clunky, and required extra willpower, thought, and intentionality to stay committed to those new endeavors, and then one day it didn't. That is what we call creating a mental map. There is a part of our brain called the hippocampus that finds its home within the limbic portion of our brain. The hippocampus takes in

2. Friedman, *Failure of Nerve*, 115.

3. Friedman, *Failure of Nerve*, 200.

all the new information and creates these maps that are vital for life and survival. When we change our surrounding we are literally disrupting our maps, and forcing the hippocampus to create new systems and maps that are no longer associated with the old ways of being that lead us to where we are.[4] As we commit to learn new information, patterns, practices, places, and relationships, and we choose which ones to learn, we are literally becoming the artists of our own future.

One of the principles I hope you are catching early on is that none of these realms of resilience—physical, mental, emotional, and relational—stand alone. Most of the time they overlap. The truth is, I believe they always overlap. You have probably noticed by now that by committing to physical resilience you are, in some way, committing to mental resilience as well. By committing to something that is new and takes physical effort, you are at the same time learning something new as well—you are developing healthy and new mental processes.

Planning for Mental Resilience

Let's get personal. Up to this point I have given you a slew of theoretical information that sounds good on paper but, as the old saying goes, is much easier said (or written) than done. We crave familiarity. Especially as we get older. Part of the frustration with developing new mental processes is that it goes against the idea that we have spent the past twenty, thirty, forty, or even fifty years learning what we know, and then feeling that we have earned the right to be the way we are. When this thought pattern is foundational to us, committing to unlearning and then learning new information feels like we are waiving the white flag of failure, like we are saying the last thirty to fifty years of our life have been a waste. This is probably the greatest lie holding us back from creating a new self. We need to remove ourselves from the realm of right/wrong. Let's get mythological. The phoenix. The phoenix is a beautiful mythical bird that reaches a point it simply burns up and becomes ash at the end of its life. It is out of the ash that the same and new are embodied in a rising phoenix. This is what is happening. Parts of your old way of being are turning to ash. They were not wrong, but their ability to carry you where you need to go has come to an end. Something new and fresh has to be resurrected and does so out of the ash of the old you. In other words, it's not that the past thirty to fifty years have been wrong, as much

4. Gonzales, *Surviving Survival*, 144.

as they have been preparation for who you were destined to be. Everything has a lifespan. We bought into the cultural lie that who we are is who we will always be, thus to leave the former realm for a new realm can feel more like failure than it does regeneration. It is your first half of life that created the foundation to build your second half of life. You didn't necessarily get it wrong; you just didn't prepare to move on. You did, as did I, get a lot wrong. We may have interpreted our purpose, ambition, definition of success, and ontology through self-centered lenses, and that has to change, but let the right/wrong dualism die. You were who you were. And who you were is foundational for who you are becoming. The worst thing you can do is try to go back to who you were (after all, look where it got you). It's time to move on. To move on you have to learn and develop new mental processes, ways of being, and practices.

I'm going to spend the rest of the chapter explaining things I have committed to learning as well as write about things I have intentionally unlearned, if you will, in order to rewrite the mental maps I live by. While I do not advocate for the compartmentalization of life, I want, for a moment, to separate these practices into several categories: learning and reading, physical fitness, and spiritual practices. I have not listed these as prescriptive categories that everyone should have, but these are my categories. Simply breaking your life pattern down into categories helps us uncover old patterns and plan for new ones. I have listed these realms simply to introduce a very intentional practice you should do as you commit to develop new and healthy mental processes.

Traditional Learning and Reading

I believe every category I have listed is healthy and needed to help us live to the fullest of our being. What you will see is that I changed the way I practiced them and how I engaged them; in short, I disrupted old patterns so that I could develop new and healthy mental processes. I am an avid reader. However, this has not always been the case. Up until I was about twenty-five or so, I hated reading. In fact, up until that point I don't believe I had finished more than five books. The fact that I have a Master's of Divinity degree would probably shock the majority of my past middle- and high-school teachers. As mentioned earlier in the book, I was a C and D student. I spent the majority of my middle- and high-school years, and the first couple years of my undergrad, believing I was stupid. While I couldn't make the grade on anything, I surrounded myself with people who were straight-A students—my brother, my friends, and my girlfriend. While this meant I hung around some pretty good kids, it was a constant reminder of my failures. I certainly was not the kid who was "going anywhere" with his life. On top of that, I married a straight-A student.

One Christmas after I was married, the women were in the kitchen talking about whatever, and Sarah's grandpa and uncle were discussing a few books and theology. I attempted to engage the conversation, and quickly realized their discussion was so far above my understanding that the "stupid" feeling from high school came rushing back in. But unlike my days in high school, I was determined to remedy the situation. I read the two books they were discussing and never stopped. In fact, if I don't have three or four books going at a time, you can assume there may be something wrong.

For the past seventeen years, reading has been part of my daily routine. Of all the books I have read (about fifty a year for seventeen years), about five of those books were stories. Everything else was theology, science, academic, and theory. I allowed a lust for bettering myself through knowledge, and the negative drive of never wanting to feel stupid again, to drive my choices, and those choices actually formed what I liked to read. Needless to say, I have learned a lot. I finished a bachelor's degree in biblical theology, as well as a Master's of Divinity degree. I did well by academic terms. All of this learning made me feel like a better person, until it didn't. None of it seemed to matter, nor remedy the depression that knocked me out of orbit.

I knew reading was valuable. I loved it. But the style of reading I had chosen to be absorbed by had let me down, and I could no longer think my way out of my problems. Here's the truth. Life isn't theological systems. Life isn't points of scientific facts. Life is a moving story. And I had failed at equipping myself to think in the way of narrative. Don't get me wrong, the type of reading I had been doing had helped a lot. It helped me think critically. It allowed me to do well in various environments. It even gave me a framework to analyze and assess my own life within my current depression. And while these types of books imparted plenty of new information into my brain they lacked the power of narrative. At the age of thirty-nine, it was time to learn how to live out the story I was called to live. Narrative helps us in developing new and healthy mental processes that go beyond informational knowledge.

I still read my theory, theology, sociology, and science books, but now I balance them with narrative. If I was to live through this story well, then I needed to submerse myself within stories. I needed to become a student of Joseph Campbell's hero's journey. I needed to reside in the depth of Dostoevsky's novels. I needed to allow myself to be swept up into the storytelling abilities of authors like Garth Stein, C. S. Lewis, J. K. Rowling, and J. R. R. Tolkien. And all of this began to create a narrative lens to not only see through, but to live through. It was the difference between learning about oxygen and actually breathing it deeply. It is the difference in learning new information and developing new and healthy mental processes.

Narrative was a literary genre that I was unfamiliar with. I had to leave the limbic realm and awkwardly stumble and grapple within the neocortex, until the language of story began to seep deep within my being and reshape the mental maps I had relied on before. While there are habits and practices we may need to let go of, I knew reading was not one of them. However, I needed to re-aim my reading initiatives so that they could assist in developing new and healthy mental processes.

There were so many times I wanted to quit and flip back to the type of reading I knew and understood simply because, for me, reading narratives was difficult. This is where a new kind of reading helped me form mental resilience. I had to use my will to stick with something that wasn't natural for me for my own development.

Physical Fitness

Not only was I not a reader, I was not an athlete. During recess, I was the one picked in the fourth or fifth round for teams. I was the one who would go long for a touchdown and be wide open, yet the quarterback knew if he wanted the ball caught, he probably shouldn't throw it to me. I was that kid.

From the ages of twelve to fourteen, I was overweight. I knew it. I didn't like it. But frankly, I liked Southern food more than I disliked being overweight. To be more honest, I liked what came easy more than I liked discipline. I also hated sports. I actually didn't hate sports; I hated the work they required and the team effort. I, unlike my brother, did not have the natural coordination nor proclivity for sports, and by the time I showed any interest in them, everyone else on the team I would have joined had been playing for years and were thus much better than I was. More than anything, I hated losing and being bad at something. Add that to the allergic reaction I had to physical work, and I had the perfect recipe for a kid who seemed to be interested in very little.

All of that would change. First, came the incident I had in the mall I refer to at the beginning of the book. Then a year and a half later, I was staying the summer with my aunt and uncle. Growing up, my uncle Steve was my idol. He represented, in my mind, what a man should be. He was successful. He had a great marriage. He was strong and good looking. He loved Jesus. By this time, I had lost a lot of weight, and went from an overweight preteen to a skinny teenager. One night his family and I went to see a late movie, by the time we arrived home, his boys were asleep in the back of the vehicle. Steve got out, walked around to the back of the Suburban, reached in, and grabbed both of his boys like they were as light as pillows, and walked in with them. That was the second epiphany. I wanted to be physically strong enough for the children that I would have one day to feel secure in my strength. My initial motivation for physical fitness was not inspired by the opposite sex, sports ambition, or popularity, but for a family I did not have yet. But that's what it took, and from that year on I have had a very regular fitness routine.

Fitness was a way to direct aggression. It was a way to stay fit. It was a way to feel healthy all the way around. If I were having a bad day, a good workout usually took care of it. If I were stressed, a hard workout out usually resolved it. Then one day, it didn't. In fact, fitness began to be a reminder of the fact I was aging. I couldn't do what I used to do. I needed more recovery time, and couldn't lift what I used to lift. Like reading, I knew fitness was really good for me. I needed it. I needed to find a way for fitness be the physical and emotional outlet it used to be, which for me meant a new routine that wasn't in my preformed mental maps.

What I did was engage in three different forms of fitness that I was not familiar with: kettlebells, jiu-jitsu, and running. Of the three, running and jiu-jitsu were the most prophetic to my current life. Long-distance running taught me that life is about the long haul. I knew that theoretically (thanks to reading) and I taught it all the time. But the way I lived proved I believed I was the exception. Running, including the subsequent injuries, became a metaphor for life. It was full of highs and lows. There were times I really wanted to run, and there were times all desire was gone, but I did it anyway. Unlike weights, I've never been fast enough to be impressive. So, unlike weight lifting, I never was good enough to be noticed, so all of my motivation had to be the run itself.

But it was jiu-jitsu that was more counterintuitive than anything. At first, I was always hurt. I was on the mats for a week or two then off for three or four. Every time my coach would tell me, "You are trying too hard. You are trying to use your strength. You are literally hurting yourself." For two years he would say this over and over, but for some reason I would not let it get through my thick skull. After all, I had twenty years of powering through that I was unlearning. I had twenty years in which it seemed like force was my friend. But now, in life and on the mats, it was only hurting me. There were so many times I wanted to quit, simply because my old way of doing things didn't work, and this is where jiu-jitsu helped me form mental resilience. I had to use my will to stick with something that wasn't natural for me in order to develop new and healthy mental processes that would produce the outcome I desired.

We are only two categories in and I hope you are beginning to see the common principle running through this. Part of building mental resilience was simply reimagining some of the things I was already doing into tools that assisted me in becoming who I was supposed to be.

I had reached a point in which some of my old habits were inhibiting me from growth. I had to learn knew mental process in different arenas of my life. At the time of this writing, my family and I were vacationing in Orlando, more specifically, Universal Studios. My oldest, Serena, and I had been talking about saving one particular ride as the ride we rode together to end the day. Before that ride, we were literally on the opposite side of the park. The plan was to ride one of the Harry Potter rides, and by our calculations we would still have thirty minutes to walk across the park to finish out our day on that final rollercoaster. Unfortunately, there was a snag on the Harry Potter ride, and by the time we stepped on to the ride we had about eight minutes before the park closed. By the time the ride was over we had about four minutes left—we had originally planned for thirty minutes give time, but now we had four minutes. Serena and I looked at each other and said, "Let's do it." We handed our stuff to Sarah and we sprinted . . . not jogged, sprinted, jumping over customers, strollers, and more. And as I was running, the thought hit me, "This is what you wanted to do all those years ago. You are doing it, and you are doing it with your very healthy and active seventeen-year-old." So, while my original motivation for fitness was negative, and while it has been transformed to the positive, it was, to say the least, serendipitous to have the ability to sprint through an entire amuse-ment park with my oldest daughter all because I committed learning a new process when it came to my physical fitness. What I wanted all those years ago in that mall, was happening.

Spiritual Practices

A few pages up, I said I was not writing these categories to be prescriptive. To be transparent, that may have been a bit of a lie. I do believe everyone should seek to encode spiritual, physical, and mental practices into their daily lives that helps them grow in health. For me, spiritual practices have always been high on my priority list. Yet, change in these spiritual practices has not. From the ages of eighteen to thirty-eight, my spiritual practices have remained relatively the same. They seemed to work for me. Then one day they didn't. For twenty years my spiritual practices were some version of what many call a quiet time and reading. In my tradition, the quiet time consisted of reading Scripture, praying, and journal writing. For those of you who have an expanded view of praying, I should probably let you know that the form of praying in the typical quiet time was more of a verbal monologue, and rarely if ever consisted of times of silence.

I'm not sure how to communicate the "until it no longer worked" part that I have said about my former spiritual practices. I'm not referring to an absence of God's felt presence. We've all felt that. Probably the best termi-nology I can use is the word "destructive." I'll refer back to the chapter on the apophatic, but recall that my spiritual practices seemed to be having a detrimental effect on me, not unlike the effect a workout might have on a person the older they get without sufficient recovery time. Meaning, there is nothing wrong with the workout or method, but as we get older we need to change up the exercises we've counted on for most of our youth. When we were younger and our body could take more stress, they actually benefited us, but now they only tear us down. That kind of destructive.

What I knew was that, like any other avenue in life, I couldn't neglect the path of spiritual practices if I wanted spiritual health. These spiritual practices at many times in my life had been paths of healing, and to re-engage them would give them the power to both take me back to my old life that I loved so much, but more importantly assist me in discovering a new and better life.[5]

5. Gonzales, *Surviving Survival*, 117.

For me prayer was always the crux of my spiritual life, and after twenty years of praying I felt like it was time for me to relearn prayer. The first thing I did was buy a few books: Thomas Keeting's *Intimacy with God* and *Open Mind, Open Heart*; Richard Foster's *Prayer: Finding the Heart's True Home*; and Mary Kate Morse's *A Guidebook to Prayer*. Each of these books discussed different styles of prayer that I had never heard of or engaged in, prayers that would force me out of my mental maps and develop new and healthy mental processes when it came to my spiritual development. After reading these and talking with former professors and spiritual advisors, I committed to a hybrid of centering prayer and meditation along with using Job 38–40 with what has been called the Ignatian method of prayer. Literally overnight, I went from using my words as the center of my prayer time to relying on silence.

This is not a prayer book, so I am not going to discuss these three methods. If you are at a place where you need to rediscover prayer, then I simply suggest you purchase the books I mentioned above and journey through them. What I want to do is describe the way I prayed. Remember, my method for the past twenty years had been me verbalizing my thoughts to God often times in the form of pleas and requests. In this new season, I would begin each morning with this Ignatian experience of prayer. While Ignatius prayed with the Gospels, I used Job, specifically Job 38–40. I did this for over a year. Every Monday, I would start with a three-to-four-verse section of the chapter I was in, and I would begin to read that section over and over, and very slowly. I would begin to picture myself talking to God in the same way Job was. I would picture in my mind the same things God was talking to Job about. I would do this until my mind cleared and I moved into the realm of silence. Then when my mind would begin to drift, I would use these texts to bring my mind back to my focus. At first, because my mind was such a chaotic mess, I couldn't truly meditate; this was my meditation. I needed a centering point, and for me it was Job. As time went on and my mind became clearer, I allowed my prayer to become more in line with the centering/meditative form of prayer. As this became more "natural," I then began to close my prayer time by praying through the Lord's prayer in an expounded fashion. This was new for me. At first, I wanted to throw in the towel. It was too much work, and mind would drift like a feather in the wind. But I stuck with it, and within three or four months I found my place in prayer again. It looked much different than the twenty years leading up to this time, but it was more life giving. At the end of the day, what I've realized is that this type of praying literally postures me first and foremost to be open to the Divine's flow in the universe rather than attempting to verbally tell God to submit to my will.

Next was Scripture. My view of the Bible had been evolving greatly over the past decade. There were times when the changes were incremental, and other times in which the changes were seismic shifts causing me to doubt my own faith. I am confident that spiritual guides in my life were the very souls that helped me embrace the fear, and come to terms with this evolution. I had come to a point where I was so tired of trying to fit Scripture in the categorical boxes that had been created and sealed shut some five hundred years ago. I had grown weary of memorizing and trying to create arguments to explain away the inconsistencies, inaccuracies, and unpleasantries. The truth was they were there; why couldn't we just let them be there? If the authors and editors of Scripture never found it necessary to do away with or explain away the inconsistencies, inaccuracies, and unpleasantries, why did we have to? Couldn't we just allow it to be the sacred text it is? Couldn't we allow these inconsistencies, inaccuracies, and unpleasantries to embolden it's sacredness? In fact, was it possible that the very inconsistencies, inaccuracies, and unpleasantries that I had once thought diluted the possibility of it being the word of God actually added more weight to the Bible being God's word. Just like this is not a book on prayer, it is not a book on rediscovering the Bible and its sacredness, so I will let it lie there.

Since I was sixteen, I found much guidance and life within the pages of Scripture. Somewhere in all of that I allowed myself to lose the life and guidance as I reduced it from a sacred text to a study book for Sunday sermons. I was ready to rediscover the sacredness of the text again. So, in the name of mental resilience, I knew I needed to step out of my old pattern and develop new and healthy mental processes when it came to scripture.

Part of my spiritual rediscovery was in finding a spiritual director. Pastor's rarely have anyone to pastor them. The folks in our denomination, as good-hearted and wise as they are, are also tied to the "success," growth, and well-being of the local church body as well. Meaning, it is difficult for them to advise us in a way that is not slightly prejudiced with the health of the church. I needed someone who was not connected to my local church body, and someone from a different faith background as myself. I chose a Franciscan priest and have not regretted it one bit. Just like this is not a book on rediscovering the Bible, nor on prayer, it is not a book on finding spiritual directors. There are plenty of resources out there for this sort of thing. I simply bring it up to talk about the way I began to rediscover the Bible. After a few sessions with Father Mark, I began to ask him to direct me in a Scripture reading diet. I explained my situation and told him what I was chasing. Up until this point I had my own self-directed plan: read the Bible through in one year, spend a year in the Gospels, spend a year in the Old Testament, read the Bible through chronologically, etc. All of these are great ideas, but I had gotten lost in the shallows of scriptural information; what I needed was to rediscover the sacredness of it all. For me this began with submitting to someone outside of myself, someone whose loyalties were not stretched between me and a body of believers I was pastoring. I still studied the Bible to learn from it and to teach it, but for this period of my life I relied on a spiritual director to guide me back through the sacredness of Scripture through the path he saw fit for me in this season.

These principals of unlearning and learning lay at the base of developing mental resilience because they were ways of developing new and healthy mental processes. As much as I could, I applied these new processes to every avenue of my life. I surveyed my life to look for patterns and methods that no longer took intentional thought. I looked for ways to unlearn these patterns and processes and replace them with new patterns and processes that demanded intentional learning on my behalf.

I have learned much through this process, but one thing I have learned is that if we are to continue to grow, we need to figure out how we can continually recreate who we are, through a regular rhythm of unlearning and learning. There is no reason for us to wait until we have a traumatic experience to build mental resilience. Our lesson in this should be to come to grips with the reality that we will never arrive at a finish line while we are alive. That would be a boring life anyway. We can always move into growth and stronger mental resilience by developing new and healthy mental processes.

Look for the places of autopilot in your life. Downshift and slow down so you can name those places. Unlearn them. Then commit to developing new and healthy mental processes so that you can grow in mental resilience.

Chapter 8: **Emotional Resilience**

One ought to hold on to one's heart; for if one lets it go, one soon loses control of the head too.

—Friedrich Nietzsche

All the knowledge I possess everyone else can acquire, but my heart is all my own.

—Johann Wolfgang Von Goethe

E motionality seems to be a sensitive subject. We, as a people, tend to fall on two ends of a spectrum rather than fight for middle ground. On one end of the spectrum are those who could be marked as overly emotional and allow our emotions run our lives. This often is seen in people jumping from one job to the next, dating the most amazing person they have ever met every time they date someone, or hearing every critique as an indictment on our character or ability. On the other end of the spectrum are those who see emotion as the weight hindering us from forward progress. We can turn our back on a friend to get a leg up. We can jump from one relationship to the next without being hurt. We can sit through a whole episode of *This Is Us* without shedding a single tear, which may be the point of no return when it comes to hard-heartedness. My point is that we have a hard time balancing emotion, and ironically too much or too little emotion can hijack the entire process in our development and healing.

The idea behind developing emotional resilience is to willfully put oneself in situations that provoke powerful positive emotions and allow those emotions to come alive. Typically, when we go through trauma the dominant emotions that course through our hearts are anger, shame, sadness, and depression; and if left unhealed they lead us to indifference. We need to fuel our hearts with powerful, positive emotions, and at this point in the journey it takes great intentionality. Why? We are creatures of habit. The older we get, the more difficult it is for us to muster up the willpower to attempt new things or engage in new experiences. We like predictability, which says a lot about our addiction to control. Most of the habits, patterns, and experiences we default to at this point in our lives have the whispers and shadows of the loss, pain, and betrayal that created the triggers that send us backward in the healing process. So, like a battered spouse, we go back to the old patterns and relationships because it is what we know. To move forward, we need the willpower to put ourselves in unfamiliar situations to elicit powerful and positive emotions.

Proclivity toward Negativity

Our brains are naturally geared toward negativity. You may not have noticed this, especially if you are not a natural melancholic. Take politics for example: think of the way we are more attracted to or at least take more notice of smear campaigns as opposed to positive ads. I experienced this just the other day. In Illinois we are known for our shady politics. We even have a term for it—"Chicago politics." Ironically, this is the place where we have figured out how to be bipartisan. If you are a politician in the state of Illinois, your party of choice says nothing of your criminal potential and your willingness to abuse power for personal gain. At the time of this writing we are coming close to our next gubernatorial race. I have personally only seen two television ad campaigns. One of those campaigns by one of the contenders is very positive. The candidate in this commercial is talking about how he is going to get Illinois working again. The other add currently on is by the incumbent, and the only add he has running is a smear ad against his opponent, linking him to Governor Blagojevich, who is in prison, along with three of his last predecessors. A few people were sitting in my living room the other day, and both of these adds came on. No one even stopped talking to listen to the positive ad, but when the negative ad came on, someone got out of their chair and walked over to the television to make sure they could hear it. Negativity drives us. Or what about the way we prefer negative rumors to positive truths. According to McConigal, if we want to be intentional about allowing positive and powerful emotions to be our guide rather than negative or self-defeating emotions, we have to put ourselves in situations in which we are experiencing powerful positivity at a ratio of three to one positive to negative emotions. This takes extreme intentionality. It seems everything in our world fights this ratio—turn on the news, read a newspaper, listen to the gossip on the street, you literally have to fight for the positive. There are some studies that show one of the major differences between couples that stay married and those who end in divorce is literally the difference of committing to positive experiences together verses staying swamped in the weighty mundane of the day to day.[1] In short, we can literally improve our marriages, relationships, productivity, spiritual well-being, and our overall health by intentionally placing ourselves in or creating environments and experiences that elicit powerful and positive emotions three times more than those that produce negative and defeating emotions.

The Art of Dream Weaving

I did not place emotions as the third on the list of resilience because it is third in order of importance, rather because the other two, physical and mental resilience, act as a strong framework for developing emotional resilience. In fact, the commitment to developing both physical and mental resilience literally acts like a dream weaver that assists us in developing our emotional resilience.

I used to say, "I can make myself do physical things, but I can't tangibly change my emotions." Well, that turns out to be wrong. The place we begin to make this transformation is in our hypnagogic state. The hypnagogic state is the liminal space between being awake and deep sleep. It is the place where remembered dreams happen.

Toward the beginning of the chapter on mental resilience, I refer to an experience in which I was the worst white belt on the jiu-jitsu mat. The techniques were clunky, and nothing seemed natural until all of the sudden it did. First, the techniques were clunky and frustrating, then they were a little less clunky and a little more fun, at least the experience and environment were fun; then, as I said, something weird happened. I would take a break and usually dream about the techniques, and the next time I was on the mat the techniques clicked. Many of us have had this experience in learning to ride a bike, rock climb, running long distance, or trying a new hobby. Once the new hobby becomes more joyful, it seems it is granted

1. Marano, "Our Brain's Negative Bias."

special permission into our dream world where the hobby, experience, or exercise is not only joyful, but executed well. It is here, in our hypnagogic state, that we experience the positive emotion of doing the new hobby or action well, even though we have not actually done it. Our desire to continually experience this euphoria that comes with learning and mastering our new hobby or technique is bonded together with the ability allowing us to seemingly move light-years ahead in our ability to execute it.[2]

This is incredible. While our minds are more biased toward the negative, our bodies or entire beings know the power of the positive. It is almost like our subconscious is a secret pathway into developing emotional resilience. Continued positive experiences gained through practices put into play through the development of mental and physical resilience use the hypnagogic state as a back door to get around our overly negative brains to help us develop emotional resilience. In other words, life breaks through!

My point is this: though our brains seem to engage the negative at a higher rate, we can conspire against this and utilize our dreams to begin to develop emotional resilience. How? Engage in new experiences, adventures, hobbies and exercises that create positive powerful emotions. These positive powerful emotions begin to find their way into our subconscious and dreams. Within our subconscious and dreams they begin to build up and influence the way we feel about our day, our life, and our experience. The more we stack up these positive powerful emotions they begin to overpower and thus drain the negative emotions of their strength and voice in our life.

More than Dreaming

We all know it is extremely difficult to let go of emotions and triggers that torment us. Sometimes it feels downright impossible. These are things we did not ask for. Often times they were created for us by someone else's choices and actions, harmful intentions, betrayal, and/or neglect. It often feels like the wounded party is the one who gets doubly punished. We did not ask for the betrayal, it was done to us. Then we are the ones to deal with the shame and pain as well as being stuck with the seemingly impossible task of true forgiveness. We are haunted with thoughts, images, and voices that turn into triggers. When we look back, we think of all the ways we may have been able to prevent it from happening in the first place. We convince ourselves

2. Gonzales, *Surviving Survival*, 138.

that had we been in more control, we wouldn't be in the situation we are in now. That may be true, but in situations like this the only value to hindsight is future prevention, but even at that, hindsight can be a very dangerous tool that haunts us. The truth is, it doesn't matter, because no matter how true our hindsight may be, we can't change it. It is now part of our psyche, and hanging out in hindsight prevents us from moving forward.

In our society, we value our ability to control things. Now layer this on top of the belief that had we been in more control we could have prevented our current state—control becomes an obsession. This obsession with control begins to fracture our internal being. Emotionally we are stuck in the past, physically we are living in the present, yet facing the future full of the anxiety that the past may resurrect itself. In order to begin to mend the part of us that is fractured, we have to let go of the illusion of control. It is the counterintuitive move of letting go of our desire to control the negative triggers and emotions that actually allows the emotional healing to begin. We rightly desire to get rid of the memories that haunt us. But often when we do this, when we are committed to ridding ourselves of the very triggers and memories that haunt us, we are actually rewounding ourselves over and over. Why? Because when we focus on the triggers and memories as a way to deconstruct them, we are still focusing on them. When these memories and triggers are focused on, we are actually empowering them. It's no different than riding down the street on our bikes hoping that we don't hit the tree to the left of the road. However, it seems we always end up hitting the tree, not because we want to, but because we are so focused on it for the sake of missing it that we actually collide with it. When we are committing to physical and mental resilience, what we are doing is taking our eyes (and mind's eye) off the tree, and intentionally directing them to something new and more positive. This continued rhythm creates new memories and emotions that slowly begin to seep into the parts of our brain that not only contains the triggers and memories, but the emotions that have been coupled with them. Without our control we begin to rewire our brains with more powerful and positive emotions, which literally disempowers the very triggers and memories that once had so much control over us. This is very different than denying the trigger or memory. It happened. It's there. We can't deny it. What we are doing is stripping the memory and trigger of its power.

Another way to say this is that we are using new experiences to create new emotions that overpower the dark emotions created from past negative experiences. We cannot undo the experience, and so at some point this has to be accepted. For me this was the most difficult part. Somewhere in my obsession with control was a fantasy that I could erase some of the past. As long as I held on to that, the past held on to me. Though we cannot erase the past, we can strip the past of its power, and to do this we have to create new experiences, put ourselves in new and unfamiliar environments, and engage in new rhythms to get out of our own head so that our emotional state is being fed by these new experiences and environments rather than negative memories. This is about becoming fully present in the current moment. Giving undivided attention and presence to what we are doing, where we are, and who we are with. In doing so, we are literally merging together what was once fractured. Let me explain.

At the sake of sounding like a broken record, I hope you are beginning to see that while I have separated holistic resilience into the categories of physical, mental, emotional, and social, in our real lives it is very difficult to do so. These categories build on each other and have so much overlap that it is extremely difficult to see where one ends and the other begins. For me, it was easiest to begin to wrap my head around how resilience works through the compartmentalization of these categories; however, in practice it was best to let them flow together. After all, we are whole beings. I say this to make the point that the practices and principles I laid out in the chapters about physical and mental resilience are actually part of building emotional resilience. In fact, if you have put the practices and principles into play, you are intentionally putting yourself in situations that provoke healthy emotions, which is developing emotional resilience!

Rather than repeating myself about new hobbies, practices, rhythms, and processes, I want to introduce another thought that helps out in developing emotional resilience (as well as physical, mental, and social resilience)—travel. I understand that several of my readers immediately allowed mental roadblocks to be raised. Typically, when we think of travel we think of the price tag. If you are like me, this time in your life led you to leaving the very occupation you had known for so long. Leaving an occupation leads to less money. It's simple math. This is where the power of priorities come into play. Here's one example. The average American spends about $1,200 a year on cable services. This does not include internet. Cable is not a necessity. I understand many of us believe it is. Some of us have never thought about it; it has been part of our life for so long that we just assume it as a monthly bill. Sarah and I have been without cable for about eight years, and we have no intention of going back. Needless to say, $1,200 a year can go a long way toward a travel budget. Another reason traveling equates to expensive for many Americans is because travel also equates to tourism, or resort vacations. Sarah and I have not stayed at a resort in over ten years in all of our travels. While staying at resorts, if you can afford it, is fine every once in a blue moon, I believe—and I realize this goes against popular opinion—that resort vacations actually rob us from the very thing travel is supposed to gift us with as well as diminishes the local culture. Needless to say, this is not a travel book, so I digress.

When it comes to emotional resilience, travel, or maybe a better word is "adventure," or new experiences, allows us to explore new people, places, and activities that are in no way tied to the memories and triggers that seem to haunt us. In fact, when we engage in adventure, we are actually moving ourselves outside of the realm that negative memories and triggers wield over us. When we adventure to new places, we are, in essence, journeying to blank canvases. We are intentionally putting ourselves in unknown and unfamiliar locations so that the current cultures, traditions, and customs begin to assist us in creating and writing new memories with these new experiences.

The road trips I wrote about in chapter 7 played this role for us. First, they were intentional. Second, they were out of the ordinary. We could not rely on past abilities and experiences. None of us had ever done this. We had not camped before, we had not cooked all our meals over an open fire, and we had never been locked in a van together for two months. We literally crafted our own experience that impacted and challenged everything about who we were as a family, who I was as an adult man, and my love for city dwelling.

This new, created experience was absent of the triggers and negative emotions from the past that were linked to environments, exchanges, habits, relationships, and skills that I dealt with and encountered on an almost daily basis. On the road trip, everything was different. Everything was new.

Extreme Situations Can Call for Extreme Measures

I am cautious about writing about this next idea. I do not want to propose the idea that it is ever good to run from our problems. It isn't good to run. Facing problems, I believe, is the only true way of getting through them. When I began practicing jiu-jitsu, I learned a very important principle on the mats that translates just as true to real life. When I was on the mats grappling, and someone would begin to put me in a hold, I would typically turn away from the problem, which always landed me in a worse situation. At the end of the match one of my coaches would always tell me, "Remember, you have to turn into the problem, not away from it." This is true in life as well. But sometimes, to retain the jiu-jitsu metaphor, sometimes the injury is so bad that it's not about turning into or away from the problem, it's about getting off the mat completely, so you have space to recover. This is what I am suggesting.

In some cases, while we don't need to run from the issues we face, we may need a way to create space to actually face those issues. Sometimes, if our networks are big enough, or if we live in a small enough town, and you literally can't change your routes and routines enough to create space from the hurts and triggers that face us around every corner, you may need to move. Again, let me stress, this is not a move to run from the past that caused this; it will run with you. I am suggesting a move to create space as a metaphorical restart button. Most of us will not have to do this, but sometimes it is the best route. Sometimes it isn't a permanent move; often it could be a move for just enough time to give you just enough space to get a better grasp on your new reality, to travel far enough down the path of healing until you are ready to re-engage. For us, we moved. The move was drastic, but I believe necessary.

As stated earlier, I am from Austin, Texas. For over the past decade Austin has been on the top ten list of something—top city for entrepreneurs, top walkable cities, top city for families, top fit cities, best city to live in, and the list could go on and on. We have been one of the, and at times the, fastest growing cities in the US. Everybody wanted to live in Austin. We didn't just live in Austin, we lived in downtown Austin. This was our city, we lived in it before it was the cool place to live and the hipsters took over. Austin, as far as I can imagine, will always be home. But I had to go. The reason I had to go was that I couldn't separate the drive that came out of the false self I had created from my rhythms, routines, and work, which in turn kept unhealthy emotions alive. In fact, after being away from Austin for about eighteen months we decided to go back for a visit. I fell right back into the self I was trying to deconstruct. It took me another month to get over the residual emotional effect of being there—speed, anger, anxiety, and my get-it-done mode—that led to my burn out, and consumed me again.

We moved to a place that is the exact opposite of Austin. Rather than being the fastest growing in the US, our new state literally had more citizens leaving than any other state. Rather than having one of the best economies, Illinois has one of the worst. Rather than embracing the future and innovation, we were in a place that was afraid of both. We moved here not because I had a dream to live here, but because I had a dream to live. And we knew that coming to a place like this would help us unlearn some of the unhealthy habits I had picked up. It would cause me to broaden my horizons in the way I saw people. It would force me to value other ways of living that I could ignore from a distance. It would put me around people who at one time in my life I may have thought were not as advanced as I was, but who I have come to realize I have so much to learn from. Ultimately, it brought us to a place of faith. Not belief—belief often has to do with an object or propositional truth—but faith, blind faith. I could rely on nothing that I was able to rely on in the past and for some reason that is exactly what I needed. And as far as job opportunities, I had plenty of them in more progressive cities, but instead of going with what I knew we intentionally planted ourselves in a new environment that helped provoke new and healthy emotions.

In Austin, the triggers were like mines in a minefield; they were everywhere. The lust for speed and accomplishment were always calling like a siren wooing a ship to crash into the rocks she is perched upon. There was none of that. The negative side to it is not unlike an alcoholic going through detox and recovery. There's a period where one feels lost and undone. I have talked about that earlier, so I will not repeat myself, but removing myself from my past context gave me the space, relationships, and rhythms I needed for a more resilient emotional system to flourish. I'm not sure if I will always live here. I can't imagine living the rest of this life without being by the mountains or city. But until then I am very content living with this new group of people that I have learned to love. I have found redemption in the faces and landscapes around me, and through them emotional healing has taken root in my life.

So, yes, sometimes emotional resilience means getting away from the people, places, memories, experiences, and contexts associated with anxiety, anger, and fear. Sometimes those things are just too embedded in our day-to-day life, and we need a change of scenery to begin to heal.

It seems to me, as we begin to move into the realm of emotional resilience we are beginning to move into the realm where our being is no longer divided, and when we cross that threshold we are on our way to becoming the person we were meant to be. Which is exactly what the examples I've used in this chapter do. Practicing events, rhythms, or hobbies that create positive powerful emotions that bypass our negative bent by getting into our dream world and reshaping our outlook; creating new adventures; or, maybe like us, you have to take the big leap. It will be hard, but it will be worth it. We are creatures of habit, and we tend to fall back into old routines if we are not intentional and careful about it. Emotional resilience is about intentionally putting ourselves in situations that provoke healthy emotions. How can you begin to do this now?

Chapter 9: **Social Resilience**

Friendship is unnecessary, like philosophy, like art . . . . It has no survival value; rather it is one of those things which give value to survival.

—C. S. Lewis

We may think that we fully control ourselves. However, a friend can easily reveal something about us that we have absolutely no idea about.

—Carl Jung

There is a common thread that runs through all of my suggestions from the previous chapters on developing resilience—people. We need people.

At the time of this writing, I had just learned of an old high school friend of mine, Michael, who had died. In high school we were very close, but when my parents divorced, we waited till I graduated and then we moved, and I never saw him again. Then twenty-four years later I received a text from another high school friend letting me know of the situation. I was stunned. Later that night, the group of guys I used to hang out with rehashed memories from over twenty-four years ago. There was a lot of laughing and remembering that was only possible because of . . . you guessed it, people, and the role we played in each other's life. That time in my life existed because of good people. Those same people who I haven't seen in twenty-four years were able to pick back up on a period of time and revive it in our memories because of who we were to each other. Since high school, while Michael and I hadn't stayed in touch, I began to build a long-distance friendship with his oldest brother, Rob. Rob and I probably have more in common and our personalities are even more similar. We both love cooking—he even owns a bakery, and is a man I admire for deciding to live life differently than the status quo. I was not able to make the funeral, but after the funeral, I texted Rob to let him know that our thoughts and prayers were with the family. He replied and said, "Thank you . . . more prayers needed. While at the funeral, Ryan's [the middle brother] house caught on fire, we are dealing with that now . . . 2018 is AWESOME." What do you say to that? Seriously, he just left the funeral of his youngest brother to attempt to salvage his middle brother's house which caught on fire while he was at the funeral. Are you kidding!? Then he followed up his text with this: "I can't tell you how important support structure is . . . People need people." He's right, the depth and fullness of resilience will never truly come to fruition without people.

I, like many others, could confess that a large part of the brokenness that led to the state I was in came from the illusion that I had bought into— I am my own man. This illusion lead to a belief in three lies: I alone can make things happen; I am in control; I don't need people. In fact, I allowed old betrayals to create in me an ethic, if I can use that word, of fearful independence. This fearful independence allowed me to justify living at arms length from anyone. I didn't want to allow myself to get close enough to anyone who could hurt me. Ironically, the pattern I created to protect myself resulted in hurting myself worse than anyone else could have. Often times when we create patterns and structures within our life to protect us from people, the result is that we end up protecting us from the life we were destined to live, because the life we were destined to live is connected to the people around us!

One of the greatest and, I believe, detrimental lies perpetuated by American individualism is the concept of the self-made man or woman. In fact, the concept of the self-made man or woman is a necessary component for a midlife crack-up. The title of this concept begins with a lie. None of us are actually self-made. In fact, the existence of our selfhood happened without any of our opinions, control, or choice. Our existence has nothing to do with choices we made. Our very existence is the result of two other people making a choice that produced us. That is how our life started.

The next twenty-plus years of our lives are shaped by guardians or parents; environments many of which we had no choice to be part of, such as our home, school, a faith community; our parent's friends; our friends (who were shaped by their parents); different parts of entertainment or lack of; and a personality we didn't choose to have. This list could keep going, but I think the point is sufficient. So even who you are now, which started from two other people's decision, has been shaped by outside forces that you had no control over. Every decision we make is a negotiation with the social, universal, and cultural laws that govern us. Almost at no point in life do we get to stand on an unbiased and uninfluenced platform and make a completely autonomous decision. Every decision we will make will not only affect us personally, it will affect those around us, and those in the future we have not yet met. This runs so deep through the fabric of our very being that many scientists and religious folk claim there is no such thing as true free will, because there are too many external and internal factors that shape the very force and affections we have that even allow us to use our will. And if there is no true free will, is there such thing as a true autonomous individual? That's for another discussion. Let's move on. What I am saying is that who we are and what we have accomplished (or failed to) is more about the relationships we align with as opposed to some illusion of being self-made.

This isn't just a human thing, this has been the code of the universe far longer than we have even been around, and we are simply products of that same code. The only reason life exists on this plane is not because of Earth's ability to stand alone as a planet conducive to life; rather, it has everything to do with varying degrees of gravitational pulls toward and against other bodies within the universe. Another way to say this is "relationship." Earth's relationship with everything else is what makes life possible. This same principle applies to the subatomic level as well. The only reason we even have cells and molecules is because groups of atoms are in relationship and those relationships created the next degree of magnitude which resulted in our living bodies. The law of the universe, from the subatomic level to the human being to the universal, is relationship not individual. And the quicker we break away from the chains of complete individualistic autonomy pontificated by the cult of the "self-made man/woman" and realize we are interdependent beings, the quicker we begin at developing the resilience to live and craft the life we were always destined to live.

The most ironic part of the cult of individualism is the belief that we as individuals always know what we want, and what we want is what is best for us. Ironically, I ended up where I ended up because I made choices out of the context of believing I knew what I wanted, and I alone knew what was best for me. Almost all choices we have made in our life that we end up severely regretting because they harm us and others come out of the lie that we always know what we want and what is best for us. In fact, how many bad relationships began with two people saying, "This is horrible, we don't want this"? Ha! None! All bad relationships began by two people thinking they knew what they wanted despite the advice being thrown at them. This is one of the reasons we need people. People help us see beyond the immediate when our emotions are wrapped up in the now and help us avoid really bad decisions that we have been deceived into believing we want. The truth is we don't always know what we want, nor do we always know the path to resilience when our vision is clouded by the events and choices that broke us. The essence of the life we live is dependent on the people we choose to be in relationship with.

Every decision I made that led me to the path of healing came out of my relationships. The key factor that sustained me through the beginning of my time here in the small-town Midwest was the new relationships I made. I was afraid of taking a sabbatical beyond three months. I was afraid of what that would do to my resume. I was afraid I might have to deal with more than I wanted to. I was afraid of reaching a point of no return. But when fear is a driving factor, we need relationships and the strength of others who aren't afraid to walk us through the night. Had it not been for the advice of others, and the belief that they may know what I need more than I did, I would not have risked a sabbatical beyond the three months, and had I not done that, I would not have stepped through the doors of liminality to find this new life.

Had I not had the advice and support of other peers and those older than myself, I would have been afraid of what was going on in me spiritually. I would have kept myself boxed in my past categories. I would have been afraid to leave the shallow end for the deep end of the pool. If I didn't have people speaking truths to me beyond my current comprehension, I would not have been able to understand what I was going through. I remember at one point, while in seminary, actually believing I was coming to a point of unbelief. I remember sitting in one of my seminary classes, between two great friends, thinking, "This must be what the process of unbelieving feels like." It was unnerving.

I think what we are seeing, and what I was going through, is that an uptick in the current population of people who are spiritual, and I'll even say religious, or who would like to be religious, cannot find solace in the limited religious jargon the church has made available to them. For many, the language much of our faith has been limited to for the past thousand years does not accurately describe what is happening in them and what they are experiencing. While this is happening, if you are like me, it feels like you are going through the process of unbelieving. The vocabulary handed down to us has in itself taken the place of the sacred rather than being what it was meant to be—a time-stamped, culture-specific attempt to define the sacredness we are invited into. In other words, language is always a temporary attempt at touching and talking about the Divine and the sacred. When that vocabulary fails our current situation and journey, that does not mean one is "losing faith" or "walking away from God," it simply means they have crossed the limit of the available vocabulary and are in search of new ways to talk about and express the sacred. When the faith community does not give permission to do this, it seems our only option is to "leave the faith" or "stop believing." We see this time and time again throughout history; the religious authorities have made the methods and language the point, rather than the fragile symbols that point away from themselves toward the transcendent. Many of us need new language and expressions to go deeper into faith. Ironically, at some time in the future, these new languages and expression will become inadequate at expressing what the Divine is doing. While initially this process feels like a movement away from God, I believe, in my deepest being, that this is actually the movement toward God. This doesn't mean we deny what we have known and experienced, it means we need the permission to build on past experiences to reach new horizons. This is a scary place to be. I believe that if I had not had my friends from Portland Seminary, my family, and wiser, older folks than myself, I would not have made it through this. I literally, at times, had to allow those around me to carry me, which is not easy for me.

This is the power of community. I have noticed a massive migration toward the search of public platforms minus accountability. At the end of the day, I believe the Divine is incarnated in Jesus, in nature, in the universe, and ultimately, as image bearers of the Divine, us. The idea of being an image bearer of God comes from the creation narrative in the Hebrew Scriptures. Here the Divine says, let "us" make humanity in "our" image.[1] What we have going on here is not a plurality making a singularity in his image; we have a plurality making another plurality in their image, meaning we are never more the image of God than when we are community. It saddens me to see this new trend, partly due to the power of social media, of people who have taken up the mantle of a public voice actually requesting

1. Genesis 1:26.

in their posts that the only folks they want commenting are those that agree with them. If, as individuals, we are willing to take up a public platform, we should not excuse ourselves from the scrutiny, accountability, and disagreement that comes with such a position. I am convinced that had I only surround myself with folks who agreed with me, I would have ended up lost. As much as I needed those who encouraged me, I needed those who spoke other opinions into me, and loved me still. The Divine is hidden within community, and this community, when submitted to, shapes us into resilient people we could not have become on our own.

Whom You Choose to Be in Community with Is Who You Become

One of the most amazing experiences I have ever had was our fifteenth wedding anniversary party. We had a feeling we were leaving Austin and wanted to send an invite out to our different networks of friends and throw a great party. We brought in an amazing caterer, hired the Jack Burton Trio for some killer music, and had the privilege of having one of our favorite breweries, Hops and Grains, sponsor us and donate some of their best brews. At one point in the night I gave a toast to my wife, in front of all those people, and I said, "Thus far in life we have accomplished everything we have ever wanted to do." I then paused, and looked out over the crowd, and said, "and we owe that to all of you, because without your guidance, love, and friendship the past fifteen years would not have been what it was." In that moment I believed every word of it, and today I believe it even more.

When it comes to choosing your community, we learned early on that who you choose to be in community with is who you become like. Of course, you help shape the community, but the community shapes you as much or more. We will never become who we are supposed to be, nor will we ever completely heal if we don't choose the right people to be with. In his book *The Last Arrow*, Erwin McManus challenges his readers to answer two questions: (1) Who is with you? (2) Whom are you with?[2]

The answer to the question "Who is with you?" literally determines how successful you will be at reaching your desired future. We need to seek out people who have similar ethics, values, and vision for life. People who live for the same dreams we live for, not specifically, of course, but generally.

2. McManus, *Last Arrow*, 147.

If you believe we are on this earth to make the world a better place, you can't surround yourself with those who believe their sole purpose is to retire big, or simply pay the bills. Surrounding yourself with like-minded people not only sharpens your edge but on days or in seasons when you want to let go of the values and principles you live by, it's these very like-minded people that hold you up and keep you on track.

If the answer to the question "Who is with you?" is important, the answer to the question "Whom are you with" is even more important. I can't think of a more life-giving activity than serving those you do life with. Think of it like a chain—there are those who are in front of you, mentoring and discipling you; there are those you journey with, who are right where you are; and then there are those who are behind you, the ones you are mentoring and discipling. When I can serve those I love with my very life and personhood, I become a better person. To watch others become better in life because I am with them only spurs and encourages me to keep at it. We've all heard it said that we learn when we are being taught, but we learn exponentially when we are the ones teaching. When we have the opportunity and grit to be for a people, we also grow and develop social resilience. This is the yin and yang or give and take of developing resilience through relationships. The truth is, our deepest relationships hold our best futures.[3]

Adventure and Physical Resilience

I could write volumes on the relationships I have had that have helped me develop resilience in life. One of those relationships was with a company and the people who make that company what it is. Above I stated that in choosing whom we are going to be in relationship with we need to choose those who are like us, but we also need to choose those we would like to become like.

I am a city person. There is no doubt. I love city life. I love the creativity that runs through the streets. I love the diversity of worldview, skin and personality that one encounters on a daily basis. The city is a current of dreamers and creators. I miss the city. However, city life had been building a stress with residual effects that I never learned to manage, or better stated, I never learned to acknowledge. Half, if not more, of winning the battle comes from naming and acknowledging the war. About five years before I began writing of this book, Sarah and I started becoming attracted to the

3. McManus, *Last Arrow*, 158.

outdoor adventure world, along with the ethics and lifestyle embodied by the folks who live this way—the spirit of adventure coupled with such a light-hearted acceptance of the here and now was envious.

For a long time, Sarah and I have believed in the importance of aligning yourself with the right people. We knew if we wanted to embody these same ethics we needed to seek out a relationship with an organization out of Austin, called Kammok, the very organization that may be responsible for helping us learn to live with adventure as a value. Kammok is an outdoor adventure company that promotes adventure made possible through their products. When we began to pursue this company, we didn't do so because we were outdoor enthusiasts, we did so because we valued the same principles Kammok valued, and we believed that if we were close enough to them, we too might learn to embody them. Kammok is guided more by their values than by their profit. Kammok exists to help people experience life-changing adventure. Not just a good weekend, but an adventure that changes your life. This is what their willingness to develop a relationship with our family has done. Kammok is guided by three main values: adventure, community, and love. I believe these three values, when embodied in relationship, rather than rugged individualism, hold the power to develop resilience in our lives for the adventure of life.

For Kammok, the outdoor adventure is like an icon for life. We could live our lives domesticated, taking the route of the preassigned cultural paths, not unlike going to a new country only to stay at a predictable resort, or we could journey off the beaten path into adventure. Adventure calls us out of our comfort zone to the place where our hearts beat faster and our eyes are open up to a much bigger world. For Kammok, the best way to do this is through community.

For us, we needed to develop a deep relationship with those who already embodied what we desired. This is the equivalent of a lantern as we trek through a dark, cloudy field. It doesn't seem to be a cultural value to admit we need people. Willfully being lead and mentored by others, I believe, is our way forward through brokenness to resilience. This takes work, and in an overly busy society it is work that is easily ignored. Our daily lives are not typically made up of folks we want to emulate. So, we need to do the hard work of seeking these folks out. There will be a price to pay—it may be financial. You may literally have to offer these folks a payment to spend time with them. It may be a cost of time. You may have to carve out time in your already busy schedule to make room for these folks to speak wisdom and guidance into your life. This may come in the form of a new friend, a mentor from the past, a company or organization that models the life you desire, or a spiritual director. Whatever or whomever it is, if you don't have this sort of relationship in your life you are thwarting your own development of social resilience.

Another reason these folks are often elusive or difficult to find is the simple fact that they are not part of our daily rhythm. They are extra. We have to break our rhythm to find them and be with them. This is why this isn't the only relationship that matters. So, while this is a necessary relationship when it comes to growth, I'm convinced that the most supportive relationship in developing resilience is the one that is, or at least should be, a part of our daily rhythms and routines—friendship.

Healing within Real Friendship

I love ancient history. I've read and studied most of the ancient creation myths. The wars between the gods and the humans. The epic battles between the various deities, which typically resulted in the birth of the earth. However, the one I enjoy the most is the one that goes rogue against the overarching mythologies—the Hebrew version. In this one, the God is not at war with humanity, but on their side. The gods are not battling each other, rather they are at work to produce a creation marked by beauty and peace. A few chapters into the story, after the rebellion of humanity, we have a unique encounter between two brothers.[4] One is named Cain the other is Abel. All the different interpretations of this ancient story are so intriguing. Are we reading a story of prehistorical man's attempt to tell how agriculture and thus the birth of civilization came into being through violence? Or are we reading a story of two literal brothers? While it is easy for biblical literalists, historians, anthropologists, and archaeologists to argue about this, we often miss the point as we lose ourselves in trying to prove a point that I don't think ever mattered to the original audience. I believe the real point of the story, no matter your interpretation, is that out of competitive jealousy, greed, and the need to be right, Cain kills his brother Abel and creates an ethic that will make its way all the way into modern business, politics, and family life.

After Cain kills his brother, a fascinating conversation between the deity and Cain takes place. This all-knowing God poses a question to Cain, a

4. Genesis 4.

question he surely already knows the answer to: "Where is your brother?" Cain responds with a very modern, Western concept—"Am I my brother's keeper?" In the Hebrew, the word "keeper" is packed full of meaning. Cain is literally saying to God, "Seriously, Abel is not my responsibility. I am responsible for me, not him. He's his own man! Do you really expect me to celebrate his life?" All of that is packed into the word "keeper." Another modern word for this is "friend." While I concur that the way we have come to define the modern concept of friendship does not correspond with the idea of "keeper," it doesn't mean our modern concept is correct. Often in our world, the idea of friendship has been reduced to folks who will simply agree with us. People who will never confront us. In fact, in our modern, overly politicized society, to disagree with someone has become equivalent to judging or hating them. In our search for friendship, we are often seeking out people who, rather than keeping us, will instead praise every mistake we make so we can feel good about ourselves. This is not what the Cain and Abel story had in mind. The deity in the story desires for us to have people in our lives whom we "keep" and who "keep" us. People who will look out for our well-being even when we can't see it. People who will celebrate us. People who will protect us even if they have to protect us from ourselves.

Let me be clear: the position of "keeper" is not one you should simply open up to anyone. That would be the same thing as opening yourself up to abuse. This position must be earned. This friendship takes years. It demands trusting the other with the deepest, darkest parts of our lives and knowing they will protect us as they know we will also protect them. It is to allow the other permission to speak the things we really don't want to hear, not because they judge us, but precisely because they love us. This requires two values: transparency and vulnerability, which in the end are key components to resilience. I have not had many of these relationships in my life, but when I have, it has made the essence of my life what it is. In Austin, we had four couples who had the right to speak into our lives, challenge us, and question everything about us and our actions. We were certainly each other's keepers. This journey to become someone's keeper is fraught with hurt, transparency, and humility. But in the end, it is all worth it!

In fact, one of the families I mentioned I personally betrayed for the sake of business. She is a realtor, and a damn good one at that. One time we were selling a house in Austin, and I made two poor moves. The first one I justified by the old saying, "Don't mix friendship and business." The second mistake I made was completely cutthroat. I had hired another realtor, who was known for his success in a particular part of town, to find us a new home, which ironically, I ended up finding. However, we offered our friend our house to sell. After hearing all the reviews on the hired realtor, I essentially "used" my relationship with my friend to "fire" her and hire the other realtor. Who does that to a friend? Apparently, me. After I made the deal, I knew I was wrong and went against every feeling in my gut. But this friend of mine cared more about our relationship and me than she did about appearing strong. She confronted me, she told me how I had made her feel. She was right. I betrayed her trust. I, like a good modern man, tried my best to talk niceties and speed up the process of healing so we could move on and I wouldn't have to face my own selfishness. She wouldn't have any of it. She would forgive, there was no doubt, but I truly hurt her. The hurt was so bad because the friendship had been so deep. It took time. I had to sit with the pain I had caused. I had to own it. This was not her being mean, this was her being my keeper. I had to work at re-establishing our friendship, and to this day this family has been the best advisors, advocates, and friends we have ever had. Why? Because this is what keepers do. Had she hidden the pain, it would have hurt her and allowed me to justify this selfish attribute in myself. I could have lived in denial of this part of myself, which would have thwarted my own development. However, she took the high road, a most uncomfortable one at that, to make me face my inner sin. I had to change. I did.

We earned this right from each other, to be each other's keepers, because we cared this deeply for each other. She would have had every right and reason to leave the relationship. But we had already invested too much. She knew I was more than my mistake. And because she knew that she would not allow me to settle for a simple surface apology; as a keeper of mine, she insisted on transformation. I never doubted her family's love for us. Our relationship only became stronger. Ironically, the gentleman I hired instead of her never sold our house, and after our contract with him ended, she sold it . . . in eighteen hours.

When Sarah and I moved to Illinois, and my depression was at its worst, it was this family, even from a distance, that listened, advised, and loved us through it. They were the first we called when we needed to talk, they were and are our keepers.

Whom do you currently have in your life that you have given permission to keep you? The long and short of it is, your journey to developing social resilience is dependent on having and being keepers. C. S. Lewis said,

"[True] Friendship is unnecessary, like philosophy, like art . . . . It has no survival value; rather it is one of those things which give value to survival."[5] While it isn't necessary for survival, it is necessary for developing social resilience. Surround yourself with people who will keep you and allow you to keep them!

Give Yourself Away

While the first type of relationship, being mentored, requires submission and humility, and the second, being a keeper and being kept, demands transparency and vulnerability, the third necessary relationship in developing social resilience is also the one that forces us into a growth pattern for the sake of others. In all my years of being mentored, fostering friendships, and mentoring and/or teaching others, I have found that I grow (and heal) the most when I am committing myself to the growth of others. In fact, every organization's future—families, businesses, religions, or clubs—is dependent on the current leader's willingness to develop those who are coming after them. As an easy example, just think about the positive snowball effect when adults take the time to mentor kids in school who will never be able to pay them back but will be able to pay it forward in society.

Forming a relationship with those coming after us or are less fortunate than us requires patience and generosity on our part. At the core of generosity is the willingness to give without the expectation of ever having a tangible return paid back to us. The more generous you are in developing those coming after you or less fortunate than you, the more you will actually grow and receive, and that is the grand paradox. The more you pay forward the more you grow as a person. This is growth mentality. Unfortunately, it is easy to develop a scarcity mentality. The difference between the two is not so much in what you have, but how you see. The root of scarcity mentality is the belief that what we have is never enough, because what we have could always be taken away from us by whatever or whomever we have been convinced to fear. Any sort of "giving" within this mindset is based on what we might get back, or what favor we could receive in the future. However, those with a growth mentality don't deny that some day for some reason all we have could be taken away from us, but they realize that, no matter how much we gain, if that which takes from us is more powerful than us, it doesn't matter how much we gain, it can still be taken from us. So, rather

5. Lewis, *Four Loves*, 90.

than hide and hoard in fear, they learn to give in generosity, and ironically, end up being the ones who gain the most.

Those of us who have been through traumatic situations that have caused us to recoil in fear, anxiety, or depression easily slip into scarcity mentality. It is a fear-based protection in which we hope we can protect ourselves from going through what we went through last time around. Unfortunately, when we live out of this mentality, we rob the world around us from the gift of ourselves, and we also rob ourselves of the gift of growth that leads to social resilience. When we do not have the types of relationships in which we pour ourselves into, we create an imbalance in our lives, which results in implosion. We have to balance out the other two relationships with a set of relationships that cost us for the sake of others. The question I have for you is, who do you have in your life that you are giving to, developing? If the goal is to develop social resilience, then we have to have all three of these relationships in our lives. And the circle of social resilience isn't complete until you are willing to develop relationships with those few people you can begin to pour into.

Hormonal Engineering

I'm sure you guessed it, but there's science that backs this up as well. While most of the great religions in the world attest to the fact that we gain more strength through community. Once again, science backs up what the great religions have known for a long time. We have learned through the study of biology that deep social interaction causes the release of oxytocin. Oxytocin is the same hormone released when we fall in love, orgasm, go through childbirth labor, or when a woman breastfeeds. This hormone imparts feeling of wholeness, joy, and well-being and promotes physical contact, which, you guessed it, releases more oxytocin. When oxytocin goes up, the stress and anxiety that feeds the triggers and past hauntings actually goes down.[6]

Increased oxytocin levels are necessary to help us develop in resilience. From the little I've learned about oxytocin, I have simultaneously noticed that when my oxytocin levels are high during a time I encounter a trigger, the trigger has much less effect and power on my well-being. In fact, it seems the higher my levels of oxytocin, the weaker the triggers.

All of this works together. If we look back throughout our life, the best memories we have were created with people. It is not lost on me that

6. Gonzales, *Surviving Survival*, 114.

many of our worst pains also come from people. However, if the best times of our lives and our best memories are created with people, then it's easy to see that creating new memories to override the memories that haunt us is going to involve being with people. When we commit to pursuing a couple of relationships with those who are further along than we are, taking current friends deeper by becoming each other's keepers, along with finding a couple of people whom we can pour our lives into, we are creating rhythms in our life that lend to increased oxytocin levels, which in the end lends to the development of greater social resilience.

Chapter 10: **A Dependable Rule of Life**

If you can't describe what you are doing as a process, you don't know what you are doing.

—W. Edwards Deming

I f you have made it this far, it is likely you are committed to developing resilience in your own life or possibly walking with a loved one through a season of liminality marked by anxiety or depression brought on by some sort of physical or emotional trauma. Unlike aging, developing mental, physical, emotional, and social resilience doesn't just happen, we must be intentional about it. I hope and pray that I didn't convey this would be easy. It isn't. It. Is. Hard! But it is worth it. It is rewarding.

In chapter 5 I discussed the idea of having a word for the year. Towards the end of 2017, I realized I was finally swimming out of the deeper waters of liminality. I was still on the liminal path, but on more walkable ground. I was moving into an unknown area while being asked to take responsibility for it. It was time for a new word for a new season. I believe there are two ways to go about this. If you lean more into the mystical dimensions of life, I believe we can simply ask for the wisdom we need that can be encapsulated in a word and trust that the word you need will be given to you through another person, an inner voice, or some serendipitous circumstance.[1] If that's not your route, and you lean more into the analytical, mark out some space on your calendar for silent reflection over the past year, and with a critical eye begin to dissect the ups and downs, successes and failures, along with fears that may have held you back. Where does life seem to be pointing you? What do you believe is on the other side of this liminal space? What idea or word(s) best defines that which is required for you to move forward and onward? Use that word as a meditation point. Use it as

1. James 1:5.

a lens or filter for decisions. Be honest. For me, the word I felt like I was receiving was "trust."

I could have probably used the word "faith," but over the years the concept of faith has lost its original meaning. It has been dumbed down to mental ascent, or a list of statements we can quote and confess. Originally faith was a lot like trust, they both dealt seriously with actual movement into the unknown. Faith, or in my case trust, is the ability and willingness to move into the unknown, or a new field, without the proof or knowledge that everything will work out. When we step on a new shore, trust is all we have. This isn't any sort of trust, this is trust pointed at a higher force, something beyond us. A force I believe to be God. Because we have not been on this shore before, we do not have previous experience to lean on. We must lean into something that is ahead of us, often something we cannot see and have not known, and this takes trust.

One of the best stories that set me up for walking onto new shores comes from the Hebrew Scriptures out of the book of Joshua. I don't want to take too much space giving the backstory to the text. But essentially, Joshua is the leader of a mass of people. For forty years they have been living in the land of liminality called the wilderness. In other words, they no longer live in their past, but they have not yet taken possession of their future; they are squarely situated in the "in-between land." It is now time for Joshua to lead these people into new territory. When we pick up the story in the third chapter of Joshua, we find the people on the opposite side of the shore they are heading toward. To get to the new shore, they are going to travel through new waters:

> Bright and early the next morning Joshua and the Israelites left Shittim and came to the Jordan. They camped there before crossing the river. After three days the leaders went through the camp and commanded the people: "When you see the ark of the covenant of the Lord your God being carried by the Levitical priests, you must leave here and walk behind it. But stay about three thousand feet behind it. Keep your distance so you can see which way you should go, for you have not traveled this way before." Joshua told the people, "Ritually consecrate yourselves, for tomorrow the Lord will perform miraculous deeds among you."[2]

This text describes the new shore as a never-before-visited location: "you must leave here . . . for you have not traveled this way before." For

---

2. Joshua 3:1–5 (NET).

many of us this may be describing our occupation. For others, a whole new chapter in life. For others, it could be describing a geographical move, or new relationships, or all of the above. The point is, these folks are heading into a new land, through an uncharted path. They are leaving what they know in order to take a path they have never traveled, to arrive in a land they have never been before. Joshua tells them to do two things: first, he tells them not to rush forward. This is often our tendency. After being in the place of liminality for so long, or being in the place where we feel lost, the moment we feel any inclination of direction, we attempt to rush headlong into it. Joshua says, ". . . Keep your distance so you can see which way you should go." If you refer back to the text, Joshua is talking about making sure the folks walk behind the the divine presence. Joshua is saying, allow the divine presence, or this guiding energy that has directed you this far, to continually lead you. Don't rush ahead of it. Let it guide you. The place this story slightly breaks down, if you are like me, is in knowing the difference between the divine presence and some internal desperation to leave your current circumstances behind. In the Joshua story, the divine presence is symbolized in a tangible item, the ark. There was no mistaking what the presence was and wasn't. Unfortunately, on the surface, we don't seem to have that tangible item. Often, the idea of following this intangible, unsee-able so-called presence scares us.

Maybe this is the first reason I believe the word for me this year is "trust." After twelve years of ministry in the organized church and three years of liminal wandering, I have come to believe that we do have the tangible presence of God in our life. Our ark, is not a golden box, rather the tactile experiences and people in our life. In fact, I believe that as we begin to practice the development of physical, mental, emotional, and social resilience we are opening our eyes to see and hear the divine presence in our ordinary existence. Interesting enough, if you read what is commonly called the Torah, the ark is nothing special in and of itself. It is a box of wood, metal, carvings, and sculptures. However, the artifacts within this box are very special to these people. These artifacts are pieces of Israel's history; they carry meaning because of what they were and are to Israel. The items help the Israelites remember times within their history when the Divine showed up in unexpected ways. We all have these. We may not have tangible items from our past, and this may be a good practice to begin. It's easy. We've all had those moments when we were on a mountain, or at a seashore at night, and we felt and heard the Divine's presence in a way that was stronger than proof. Many of us journal about that experience. Some of us look around in that moment and pick up a rock or stick or some item that will help us recall the power and beauty of that moment. To most people, like the artifacts within Israel's ark, they contain nothing special, but for us they are holy elements, elements that remind us of something God did as well as point forward. As far as the ark itself, the only thing that made it special was the fact that the divine presence had decided to rest up on it. Like the holy elements, I believe we all have an "ark" in our lives, an ark that carries with it the divine presence. Instead of being made up of wood, metal, and other earthly materials, our "ark" is made up of people, landscapes, and movement. Unfortunately, many of us choose to see these elements as expendable, thus never realizing that these elements are often conduits for the divine presence, a presence that is leading us to new and better shores.

I will not take the time to develop the idea of people as conduits of the presence of God, as I did most of this in the previous chapter dealing with social resilience. I will just say this: in the creation myth of Genesis we have a deity that makes its image visual by imparting the divine presence into a people—not a person, people. This same trajectory carries itself from the first story of the Hebrew Scriptures into the Christian teachings of the New Testament. While at times, we need to get away in times of silence in order to decipher where and how the presence is leading us, we are never more in the presence of the Divine than when we are around people who are seeking the same presence. Allow me to add a caveat. Again, I refer to the previous chapter for a more in-depth explanation, but in our society it seems common place to surround ourselves with people who will only validate our every move and decision rather than challenge us. It seems to me, in pursuit of these types of "friendships" and Western comforts, the greater goal of life is to avoid tension at all costs. On the surface, this sort of comfort structuring makes sense. We all live with an inner drive to find peace.[3] However, like many of our pursuits of pleasure, we settle for the quick easy way rather than the higher path. Those of us who have lived long enough know that the quick easy way never delivers what it promises. Never. Fortunately, or unfortunately, depending on your point of view, the peace that we all seek, the peace that is promised to us from God, is not absent of tension, but often found in the midst of it. In fact, I was sitting in my spiritual director's office the other day, and he told me, "Matthew, as a whole we often believe the peace of God is found in times absent of tension,

3. Job 3:25–26 (NET).

but I don't think you can point to a single example of that anywhere in Scripture or in church history. The ironic thing is, when we attempt to structure our lives to avoid tension, we are at the same time structuring a life void of peace as well—it leaves us hollow. What you do find, however, is the peace offered to us by God is often and maybe even only found in the places of tension." This is true with our relationships as well. When we surround ourselves with people who see the world the way we do as well as those who see it differently, we are setting ourselves up to better know the presence and direction of the Divine in our lives. I believe this is the first step in creating our tangible "ark." We are shaped and directed by these relationships.

If the first element in our "ark" is in friendship and relationship, the second is in landscapes. Nature. One of my favorite professors at Portland Seminary calls nature "God's second book." To some, this may sound heretical, but I believe he is in pretty good company to do so.[4] I believe this is an entire truth that has been missed by the Western church, mainly out of fear. In missing this, we have missed the God who laced creation with his moving presence. One of my favorite texts about this is in one of my favorite books in the Hebrew Scriptures, Job:

> But ask the animals, and they will teach you;
>
> the birds of the air, and they will tell you;
>
> ask the plants of the earth and they will teach you;
>
> and the fish of the sea will declare to you.[5]

This is one of the most quintessential ideas modern psychologists, adventure junkies, and sociologists seem to be communicating to us for the purpose of health—get unplugged and get immersed into nature. Something happens in and to us when we detach ourselves from the noise pollution created through our busyness. In fact, some say it takes an entire three full days of noise detachment for our brains to reboot and begin to think and hear clearly again.[6] To hear the Divine in our natural landscapes demands we commit to the process of submission. Our world tells us to hurry. Thanks to text, email, social media, microwaves, and air transportation, we have essentially removed waiting from our everyday equation. As

---

4. Genesis 9:1; Psalm 19:1; 33:5; 95:4–5; 96:11–12; 104:24–25; Isaiah 43:20; Romans 1:20 (NET).

5. Job 12:7–9 (NET).

6. Williams, "Call to the Wild."

a society we are not good at submitting to a slow process. The idea that it may take us three days to clear out our brain in order to hear and feel the Divine is enough for many of us to ignore this portion of our "ark." We have to remember, the Divine speaks in a still small voice, and the speed at which we live almost guarantees we cannot hear this directional voice over and above the noise pollution that invades all of our senses.[7] If the text I shared above is correct, and I believe it is, the ark that we seek for directional purposes and peace of mind is made up of the people and the natural landscapes that surround us; we just have to be willing to move slow enough to hear and experience it.

Finally, I believe the third element to our ark is movement. Yes, it seems contradictory to place the idea of movement after a few paragraphs promoting slowness. Movement does not have to be fast. It can be slow, fast, or somewhere in between, and movement even has its point of resting, but even in our rest and stillness, we are resting and being still at certain points on the path we have been moving along. We rest so we can move. Movement has been the constant of the universe. Since its explosion and conception, the universe has been moving outward and forward. Everything that makes up the universe is in motion. Every cell, atom, and molecule that makes you is also moving. If the God who created this universe has planted the divine presence within a moving creation and a moving people, then it would make sense that movement is every bit a part of our tangible ark. In fact, in the Joshua story, the presence that is being followed is a presence that is moving. This is where it can get tricky, because more often than not we think we know better than the presence of God, which results in an attempt to get out ahead of it, and confuse the movement of the presence with the movement caused by anxiety. I believe the key here is about keen observation as we are moving. The divine presence is revealed to us as we are taking steps of trust (aka, faith), or as we are moving, not when we are doing nothing (resting and doing nothing are different, one leans toward lazy, the other is situated within intentionality).

I understand the idea of finding and following the divine presence within people, landscapes and movement is still unsettling for many. It can be an unnerving reality to simply leave it here. I get that, I really do. Personally, I can become easily paralyzed because of the fact that I question everything. So, to that point, I have two responses: if we don't leave it here, we will never learn to truly trust our way forward, and thus remain stuck, we must trust

7. 1 Kings 19:11–13.

that some deep, primal, inner-wisdom will guide us in our relationships, contexts, and movements. The second point is that following the presence is not the only thing Joshua commands the people to do.

The other action Joshua commands of the people is to "ritually consecrate yourselves." In the original Hebrew, the idea of ritually consecrating oneself simply means to create or submit to rituals or to prepare oneself by committing to a set of practices. In other words, it is the ritual consecration that allows us to know, see, and hear the presence of the Divine in people, landscapes, and movement. The ritual consecration creates in us an ability to decipher and intuitively know the difference in the voices we are hearing. In this incident, and for me, the idea of ritual consecration would mean to create or submit to daily practices or rituals that help build resilience in our lives, which will guide us to and through the new land. The reason we need to do this is that it is so easy to get side-tracked or allow the new journey to get hijacked by everything from busyness to fear to conflicting messages coming from our immediate culture. In fact, Joseph Campbell said, "A ritual is the enactment of a myth. And, by participating in the ritual, you are participating in the myth. And since myth is a projection of the deep wisdom of the psyche, by participating in a ritual, participating in the myth, you are being, as it were, put in accord with that wisdom, which is the wisdom that is inherent within you anyhow. Your consciousness is being re-minded of the wisdom of your own life. I think ritual is terribly important."[8] Remember, "myth" does not mean fake. Often, throughout civilization, the word "myth" means something that is so true it is difficult to compress into systematic statements, and must be expressed in stories and lived-out experiences. Your own lived-out reality and future trajectory can be told and should be seen as a real mythical journey.

In the second to last line, Campbell says that through ritual enactment "your consciousness is being re-minded of the wisdom of your own life." Just two paragraphs ago I closed out writing about following the divine presence as a way of trusting your inner, primal wisdom, which coincides with what Campbell, and, I believe, Joshua are saying: we need to enact rituals in our lives that keep us in line with our interior wisdom that has been developed or revealed as we have developed wholistic resilience. These rituals keep us on track with the myth that is calling us forward so that we are not lured away by everything else around us.

8. Campbell, *Power of Myth*, 228.

I would like to close out the book by talking about the plan I have put in place for my life. I do not wish to add another box to check on our to-do list, rather I would like to assist you by giving you an example of how I used intentionality to rearrange many of the things in my life that already existed to create rituals that have been beneficial in the daily development of resilience, which has resulted in the ability to move forward into these uncharted waters rather than remain paralyzed by the unknown.

Rule of Life

The ancient monks had a practice they called a "rule of life," or, to use the above language, which I am now departing from, daily practices of "ritual consecration." A rule of life is simply a rhythm of intentional rituals or practices designed to help us stay on a path toward wholeness and resilience. To use a sports metaphor, this is not different than training for a marathon. If running twenty-six miles is our goal, we can't expect to simply wake up one day and just do it. We have to begin to reorient the way we eat, think, train, and rest in order to accomplish what we want to accomplish. Laurence Gonzales refers to this same idea when he talks about keeping a posture of anticipation. Anticipation is essentially the willingness and ability to begin to actualize our desired future, through a daily commitment of practices. In other words, these practices help us begin to bring the vision or myth that we can only see in our hearts into reality. When the vision or myth is seen clearly in our mind's eye, we then back into that vision by putting daily practices into place in order to develop within us the daily resilience required to stay the course when that anticipated future is coming under threat by downfalls, trauma, or the like.[9]

What I am about to share is my own personal rule of life. I have categorized my practices based on the four types of resilience we have discussed in the second half of this book—mental, emotional, social, and physical. When I have showed this to other people, they have been surprised that I have not had a category dedicated to the spiritual. So, allow me a moment to explain. I do not believe the spiritual is a category among others within our humanity. I believe everything is spiritual. To be dedicated to spiritual health is the same as being dedicated to the mental, emotional, physical, and social health; just as being dedicated to mental, emotional, physical, and social health is being dedicated to the spiritual. In other words, everything is spiritual. To separate

9. Gonzales, *Surviving Survival*, 205.

the spiritual from everything else as a lower or higher dimension is to take on the very gnostic posture that the church spent the first four hundred years of its existence fighting. So, while spiritual does not get its own category, I believe all the categories are spiritual.

Before I display the actual practices, I want to add a single caveat. Vision. You will notice that these practices, while in some cases are general, they are not random. I have been, and possibly still am, in the place of liminality. I have (as have you) left one shore for another. We have a vision of the other shore even if we have not traveled to that shore. If you do not have a vision of the next shore, I recommend you take a few days or weeks or months to pray and think about your vision. Let me say this in another way: the idea of vision is often polluted with ideals from the me-centric corporate world. That's not what I'm talking about. I am talking about answering the question, "Where do you see yourself in five years?" You know as well as I do that there will be places along the way where that vision may change or you may have to make course corrections, or you realize the vision is too small. When this or if this happens, some of your practices may be altered as well, because the practices within your rule of life are informed by your vision. These practices are leading you to the place where your myth is your reality.

So, for example, if I can be transparent again, in five years I see Sarah and I running a new business dedicated to local, social, economic, and cultural renewal. I see this business as a faithful presence reflecting kingdom values within an alternative society. This business will give a percentage of its profits back to education, social, and community development programs within its county of influence. Most of all, we are creating a community-wide vibe that is helping people realize they can be a force of good through their everyday common actions . . . or as we like to say, "We are helping people live ordinary well." Through this I see that Sarah and I have started a new small alternative faith community, which looks more like the Emmaus journey out of Luke 24 than it does an institutional church!

That's it. While I have an idea as to what this business may be, I'm not sure yet. What I do know is that the vision above could be describing several different options. I'm not nailing myself down by being too specific, but I am defining a vision for where I want to be in five years. The following is a list of practices that I believe help me stay on track with the above vision, while at the same time submitting that vision, through daily ritualistic practices, to God. These practices are categorized into the four dimensions of resilience: physical, mental, emotional, and social; they are also categorized into daily, weekly, monthly, and annual practices.

In My Daily Life

I commit to daily fitness as a means of developing and sustaining *physical resilience*. I do not know the demands the future will have on my body, or the adventures I will choose to embark on, but I do know I want to be physically able to embark on those expeditions, especially when the drive behind those adventures or expeditions is for the sake of physical resilience. I also realize that a healthy body is connected to a healthy mind and life and therefore committing to a physical fitness routine that makes future endeavors possible. As for the daily development of *mental resilience*, I will commit to reading (book or blog) on subjects I desire and need to know more about as well as engage in process-oriented hobbies that allow me to develop a more mature and healthy mental process. In the way of daily developing *emotional resilience*, I commit to twenty-three minutes of lectio divina and/or meditation a day. I find these practices not only assist in developing healthy mental process but they assist in developing the ability to direct my emotions in a healthy direction. One's emotional maturity is often displayed not so much in how one handles successes, but rather in how one deals with challenges. Different challenges elicit different emotions. For this, I commit two hours a day, five days a week, to moving the needle forward in our new business endeavor. This practice will force me to encounter both successes and failures, which will in turn cause me to see where my emotional intelligence lies. Finally, as a highly driven introvert, I cannot neglect the daily development of *social resilience*. I must be honest with myself about the difference between working to accomplish something and working as a way to ignore the demands around me. Therefore, I commit to finishing all my work by 4 p.m. Monday through Wednesday. This includes the answering of phone calls and emails for business purposes, or any sort of planning that removes my full attention from my friends and family. As you can see, these are not earth shattering practices. The power within them lies within the intention behind them. And the intention behind them is what helps me develop resilience for the future.

On a Weekly Basis

The following paragraph is a description of the commitments I make on a weekly basis that reflect the categories of resilience displayed in the previous chapters. When it comes to the weekly development of *physical resilience,* weather permitting, I will engage in a physical endeavor that includes fun with friends and family—a long bike ride, playing at the park, or swimming. This will allow me to incorporate both functional fitness and valuable time with those I love. To develop *mental resilience,* each week I spend a two to-four-hour block reflecting back over my work week and honestly grading it against my vision for a better future. Since mental resilience is about developing new and healthy mental process, this exercise is about setting time aside to analyze and correct the mental processes I used the week before. The result of this time will inform the actions of the subsequent week. As for *emotional resilience,* I commit to thirty-six hours of Sabbath or rest, usually from Sunday afternoon until Tuesday morning. When possible, I will figure out how to spend a portion of this time out in nature. Finally, as for developing *social resilience,* I will attempt to introduce myself to a new event or an outing with friends that demands I step out of my favored introversion for a short period of time.

My Monthly Rhythm

The following is a list of practices I fit into my monthly rhythm that reflect the resilience categories within my rule of life. Unlike developing *physical resilience* on a weekly level, on a monthly level I will look for something that is not easy-access play and engage in that. This could be anything from rock climbing, skiing, visiting a different city, to engaging in a physical activity that is foreign to me. As for developing *mental resilience,* I will carve out space to re-evaluate what I am learning and where my learning energies are directed, to grade whether or not they are strengthening new and healthy mental processes in the way I pray, play, work, and relate with others. I will be honest about this and make changes where necessary. As for developing *emotional and social resilience* on a monthly basis, I combine the two into what is famously called "date night." The most important person to me is my wife, Sarah. She is intricately involved in all the workings of my life, and it is easy for a couple to allow their relationship to slip into a functional partnership, especially when they work together. If the emotional and interrelational status of us together, as one, is not healthy, then nothing else will be. These date nights allow us the space to reconnect as husband and wife, rather than simply father and mother or business partners. Being business partners and father and mother are intricate to our identity, but before we were those, we were lovers and friends, and monthly date nights not only reminds us of this reality but gives us the tangible space to reconnect as that. Again, we see that these are not earth shattering practices. These are things many of you already do. But even when we do them on a regular basis, it is very easy to go into auto pilot. As explained in many of the chapters on the different types of resilience development, it is when we go into auto pilot that things can lose their significance strength. Those of us who are married have seen this happen with date night. Though we may have it on our calendar, it is easy for it to become hollow. Adding the intention to it, and being mindful of that intention is what allows the practice to develop depth and resilience.

An Annual Rhythm

Finally, I believe, at least for me, having long term goals that are part of re-silience development are very important. The following is a list of practices I fit into my annual rhythm that reflect the categories within my rule of life. For physical resilience on an annual basis, I seek to complete in one or more physical challenges—i.e., a long run, bike ride, or competition. Do you see the cyclical nature of this? This annual goal now informs my daily and weekly practices. In fact, as I write this Sarah and I are actively looking for a competition of sorts that will take us out of our physical norm, take on new practices, which ultimately strengthens physical resilience. As for *mental resilience*, I will attend a seminar, workshop, or conference that undergirds my prayer, play, or work life, that will awaken, remind, or challenge me to seek out new and healthy mental processes for all my activities. For *emotional resilience* I will commit to some sort of spiritual retreat or time of solitude. It is my goal, to carve out a two-day prayer retreat each year in a place of solitude. As I write this, a friend and I are planning a silent retreat at the Abby of Gethsemani. Committing to silence for three days elicits a slew of emotions. Finally, in the way of social development, as mentioned above, the arena that I am committed to first and foremost is the social order of my family. So yearly, to develop *social resilience*, I commit to a family and couple vacation, one of which includes being in nature, rest, exploration, and/or adventure.

Some of you may be thinking that you already do a lot of this. I did too. But I wasn't as intentional as I am now. My intentionality has infused my practices with deeper meaning. For much of my life, as stated earlier, I have practiced spiritual disciplines, but like many of you the discipline ended up being about the discipline; I had allowed the practices to become disconnected from a vision. This is why I start this process with identifying and writing down a vision. A dear friend of mine, Jennifer Williamson, was instrumental in helping me see through the lens of a "rule of life." I will not be attempting to use her analogy, but she does a great job of explaining how each part of one's life is like the room of a house: for the house to be in good order and healthy, each room needs attending. The house becomes whole from the inside out. Often times our old discipline paradigms keep the outside looking good but neglect the inside. Simply adding intentionality and meaning to many of the practices I already had in play allowed them to affect me at a deeper level. We have to remember a part is not its own autonomous part, it is part of the whole, and without being connected to the whole it loses its value and importance, which is why when it comes to developing a rule of life that creates and sustains complete wholistic resilience we must be as committed to physical resilience as we are to emotional resilience.

Some of you may think, "Whoa! This is a lot." That's okay, I am often criticized for trying to take on too much, and the critics are often correct. Start smaller. It's not a competition. It's about being the best you that you can be. What I can tell you is that you will not just wake up the way you want to be; you have to be intentional about creating you each and every day. There will come a time when you are challenged to the very core of your identity, and if you have not been preparing yourself for that challenge it will be very difficult to come through. A rule of life, while it won't always allow you to dodge the attack, trauma, or incident, will prepare you to handle these different seasons of life with resilience, so you can actually grow through them rather than lose yourself.

What's Next?

So, here we are. We've walked through this state of liminality. We are stepping into uncharted territory. I don't know what tomorrow holds for you or, for that matter, me. What I do know is that to find it we have to adventure toward it. We have to risk. We have to take chances. We have to step into the fog. We have to drown out the noise and listen to the voice that calls us forward.

Over fifteen years ago I had the opportunity to be the personal guard and assistant to the late Brennan Manning for a weekend conference he was holding at a church in Illinois. This was an amazing opportunity for someone like me, at the beginning of their ministry journey. One thing that was peculiar to me, something I didn't fully understand, was the blessing he would give at the end of each of his sessions. After fifteen-plus years of ministry, burnout, darkness, and disillusionment, this blessing has made more sense, if not perfect sense. Brennan claimed this blessing to be Franciscan, but all I can find is that it may have been prayed over Henri Nouwen by a spiritual mentor of his. No matter who wrote it, I think it appropriate for you and me as we begin to write the next chapter in our journey:

May all your expectations be frustrated.

May all your plans be thwarted.

May all your desires be withered into nothingness.

That you may experience the powerlessness and the poverty of a child and sing and dance in the love of God the Father, the Son, and the Spirit.

Epilogue: . . . Since Then . . .

There is nothing like looking, if you want to find something. You certainly usually find something, if you look, but it is not always quite the something you were after.

—J. R. R. TOLKIEN[1]

A pastor friend of mine, actually one of the men I had the opportunity to plant a church with, Brandon Hatmaker, used to say something to the effect of, " . . . I just want to hold things with an open hand." In reality, this is a difficult yet noble way to live. Through my experiences, I have found those who want to hunker down and protect their little corner of the world, are at the same time protecting themselves from the growth, beauty, and adventure the world around and beyond them has to offer. I have also found there are those whom are willing to hold life with an open hand, or at least attempt to. Those of us who attempt to live with open hands release ourselves to change, progress, and the unexpected, which leads to adventure, growth, and fulfillment beyond what we could have achieved on our own.

For over fifteen years in Austin, my family and I have lived a good life pastoring with some really great people, but, as laid out in this book, I allowed myself to get swallowed up, burned out, and pitched into the mires of depression and disillusionment. I allowed misinformed resentment and anger to become the lens that obscured my vision of many around me, and eventually closed the hand that was I attempting to hold open. The irony of holding life with a closed hand is that one often gets lost within the very self or world they were trying to protect.

This book has laid out how I, using resilience theory, mentors, and the love of friends and family, climbed out of this dark hole. I attempted to communicate how the Divine was using this brokenness as a pedagogy of

1. Tolkien, *Hobbit*, 65.

undoing and remaking, an undoing that would prove to be the path of re-making me into my true self. As I climbed out and began to look for a new way to live, a new form through which to express my vocational identity, I assumed healing meant finding my way back to my initial life of pastoring and church planting. However, when one is committing to hold life, includ-ing the very city and job they have known for all of their adult life, with an open hand, many times the way forward may not be a recovery of what was.

I initially assumed true healing meant getting back to what I was doing before, but much like the Tolkien quote above, what I found was not the something I thought I was after. It was better. Since the writing of this book, the Hansen family, rather than living in larger progressive cities, where we are most comfortable, landed in a small rural community in west-central Illinois. Rather than pastoring an institutional church, we have started a brewery! Our lives look more monastic than they do pastoral. We have many people ask about our change of occupation and location. "Why would someone come to a place like this?" is often the sad question echoed by long-time citizens, or "Wow, from pastor to brewer, that's a change." We come to a place like this because, amidst all the pain and loss the rural Midwest has experienced over the past several decades, it remains a place of promise, hope, and beauty. The change from pastor to brewer is only a change in form; the vocational drive is the same. We desire to be a voice of economic, social, personal, and community development that models the kingdom. In Austin that looked like a pastor, here it looks like a brewer.

Will I ever pastor again in a traditional or institutional church? I don't know. I do miss it. I love speaking. I love stirring new ideas. I love confes-sion. Little did I know that being a brewer would allow much of this in a less guarded way. So, though I'm not a Christian church pastor, I am slowly becoming a spiritual guide to many who do not consider themselves reli-gious or Christian—kind of a people's pastor. I've always longed to live by the mountains. Will I ever get to answer the call of those mountains, to live by them? I don't know. Maybe I will have the opportunity one day to settle down around the mountains my heart longs for. But that's not today. Today we are here. We are planted, and committed to Knox County, Illinois. We get to be a part of a beautiful people and landscape. We get to model a new way of business. A way of business that is very kingdom-esque. A way of busi-ness that attempts to be a voice in creating local economy. A business that prioritizes well-being above bottom-line profit. A business that hopefully expands the meaning of value, economy, and trade. A business that trusts that as it seeks first the good of the county we are in, we will also find our own well-being within it. A monastic way of doing business. But most of all, we get to be on an adventure in a very ordinary life, in a very normal place, that allows us to live very intentional lives, among a very beautiful people; or something our family likes to say: "We get to live ordinary well!"

Bibliography

Beachy-Quick, Dan. "Apophatic." *Verse Daily*, 2016. http://www.versedaily.org/2016/apophatic.shtml.

Beech, Nic. "Liminality and the Practices of Identity Reconstruction." *Human Relations* 64/2 (2010) 285–302.

Belletete, Jonathan, and M. B. Paranjape. "On Negative Mass." *International Journal of Modern Physics D* 22/12. (2013) 22.

Campbell, Joseph. *The Hero with a Thousand Faces.* 3rd ed. Novato, CA: New World Library, 2008.

Campbell, Joseph, Bill D. Moyers, and Betty S. Flowers. *The Power of Myth.* Logan, IA: Turtleback, 2012.

Chandler, Diane. "Pastoral Burnout and the Impact of Personal Spiritual Renewal, Rest-taking, and Support System Practices." *Pastoral Psychology* 58/3 (2009) 273–87.

Dostoyevsky, Fyodor. *The Brothers Karamazov.* Translated and annotated by Richard Pevear and Larissa Volokhonsky. London: Vintage, 2008.

Friedman, Edwin H., Margaret M. Treadwell, and Edward W. Beal. *A Failure of Nerve: Leadership in the Age of the Quick Fix.* New York: Seabury, 2007.

Gonzales, Laurence. *Surviving Survival: The Art and Science of Resilience.* New York: Norton, 2013.

Hunter, James Davison. *To Change the World: The Irony, Tragedy, and Possibility of Christianity in the Late Modern World.* New York: Oxford University Press, 2010.

Huxley, Aldous. *Ape and Essence.* New York: Harper, 1948.

Johnson, Jan. *When the Soul Listens: Finding Rest and Direction in Contemplative Prayer.* Colorado Springs, CO: NavPress, 1999.

Ledbetter, Carly. "One Guy Figured Out How to Plan the Best Road Trip Ever." *HuffPost*, March 15, 2015. https://www.huffpost.com/entry/plan-a-road-trip_n_6839764.

Lewis, C. S. *The Four Loves.* San Francisco: Harper One, 2017.

———. *A Grief Observed.* San Francisco: HarperSanFrancisco, 2001.

———. *Till We Have Faces: A Myth Retold.* New York: Harcourt, Brace, 1957.

Marano, Hara Estroff. "Our Brain's Negative Bias." *Psychology Today*, June 20, 2003. https://www.psychologytoday.com/us/articles/200306/our-brains-negative-bias.

McGonigal, Jane. "The Game that Can Give You 10 Extra Years of Life." TEDGlobal, June 2012. https://www.ted.com/talks/jane_mcgonigal_the_game_that_can_give_you_10_extra_years_of_life.

———. *Super Better: A Revolutionary Approach to Getting Stronger, Happier, Braver, and More Resilient.* New York: Penguin, 2015.

McGrath Davis, Brian. "Apophatic Theology and Masculinities." *CrossCurrents* 61/4 (2011) 502–14.

McManus, Erwin Raphael. *The Last Arrow: Save Nothing for the Next Life*. Colorado Springs, CO: WaterBrook, 2017.

Meek, Katheryn Rhoads, Mark R. McMinn, Craig M. Brower, Todd D. Burnett, Barrett W. McRay, Michael L. Ramey, David W. Swanson, and Dennise D. Villa. "Maintaining Personal Resiliency: Lessons Learned from Evangelical Protestant Clergy." *Journal of Psychology and Theology* 31/4 (2003) 339–47.

Merton, Thomas. *New Seeds of Contemplation*. New York: New Directions, 2007

Mitchell, R., and F. Popham. "Effect of Exposure to Natural Environment on Health Inequalities: An Observational Population Study." *The Lancet* 372/9650 (2008) 1655–60.

Moore, Melinda, Philip Gould, and Barbara S. Keary. "Global Urbanization and Impact on Health." *International Journal of Hygiene and Environmental Health* 206/4–5 (2003) 269–78.

National Park Service. "Healthy Parks Healthy People: 2018–2023 Strategic Plan." June 2018. https://www.nps.gov/subjects/healthandsafety/upload/HP2-Strat-Plan-Release -June_2018.pdf.

Palahniuk, Chuck. *Fight Club*. New York: Henry Holt, 1996.

Rohr, Richard. *Everything Belongs: The Gift of Contemplative Prayer*. New York: Crossroad, 2003.

Rohr, Richard, and Joseph Martos. *From Wild Man to Wise Man: Reflections on Male Spirituality*. Cincinnati: St. Anthony Messenger, 2005.

Rollins, Peter. *The Idolatry of God: Breaking Our Addiction to Certainty and Satisfaction*. New York: Howard, 2013.

Sundquist, K., G. Frank, and J. Sundquist. "Urbanisation and Incidence of Psychosis and Depression: Follow-Up Study of 4.4 Million Women and Men in Sweden." *British Journal of Psychiatry* 184 (2004) 293–98.

Tolkien, J. R. R. *The Hobbit, or, There and Back Again*. London: Houghton Mifflin, 2001.

Turner, Victor Witter. *The Ritual Process: Structure and Anti-Structure*. Ithaca, NY: Cornell University Press, 1982.

Williams, Florence. "Call to the Wild: This Is Your Brain on Nature." *National Geographic*, January 2016. https://www.nationalgeographic.com/magazine/2016/01/call-to-wild/.

Wiman, Christian. *My Bright Abyss: Meditation of a Modern Believer*. New York: Farrar, Straus and Giroux, 2013.

CPSIA information can be obtained
at www.ICGtesting.com
Printed in the USA
JSHW011719040919
1228JS00003BA/7